THE WASP MYSTIQUE

THE
·WASP·
MYSTIQUE

by Richard C. Robertiello, M.D.
and Diana Hoguet

DONALD I. FINE, INC.
NEW YORK

Library of Congress Catalogue Card Number: 87-46024
ISBN: 1-55611-062-6
Manufactured in the United States of America
10 9 8 7 6 5 4 3 2 1

This book is printed on acid free paper. The paper in this book
meets the guidelines for permanence and durability of the Committee on
Production Guidelines for Book Longevity of the Council on Library Resources

7142622

The authors would like to express their
appreciation to Donald I. Fine, our editor
and publisher, to Don Congdon, our agent,
and to Ms. Lucy Smith and Stephen L. Day
for their many helpful suggestions and
ongoing support while we were writing
The WASP Mystique.

·CONTENTS·

CONTENTS

8

·INTRODUCTION·

WASPs, as most of the world knows, are White Anglo–
Saxon Protestants. The acronym is part of the language.
They're an historic majority in our national population. No
one bothers to single them out and label them—whoever
heard of a WASP-American?—because they typify what's
perceived best and most to be desired and imitated by all
Americans. A small town merchant in Iowa is not likely to
be singled out and called "the WASP" by his fellow towns-
people the way his Jewish counterpart would be singled out
and called "the Jew." To be a WASP is to be *unconditionally*
accepted as an American. However, to *personify* a WASP is
often to be caught up in an archaic doctrine and to live one's
life as a symbol without ever becoming a real person. Many
people, WASPs and non-WASPs, have taken on this role,
often without it being a conscious choice. It is adopted early
in childhood when there is little or no awareness of relative
values; little or no evaluation.

The WASP we are concerned about is not only a person

but an attitude. This attitude may not be *overtly* expressed by the majority of Americans but it's nevertheless infectious and not confined to its own ethnic boundaries. Indeed, it is endemic.

For example, a young man in college was determined to become a WASP. It was obvious that he could never actually become a White Anglo–Saxon Protestant because he was black. He was worried that he would be held back from his goals because of his race and he thought the easiest way to downplay his ethnicity was to associate himself with WASPs. He pledged a fraternity filled with graduates from northeastern prep schools and went to all the "right" parties on campus as well as off campus. He spent a small fortune at Brooks Brothers on dozens of shirts which all looked identical and got himself a job on Wall Street. He was driven by the feeling that he could never quite master the role to perfection. He once let on after several gin and tonics that his greatest fear was that people would think he was trying too hard and that he wished he could feel "worn in" like the rest of them. Many years later it is impressive how "worn in" this man has become. His sensitivity to what it really meant to be like a WASP gained him the long sought after attitude he so prized. His was a rare case of somebody who consciously had successfully adopted a WASP persona. But he was not, never could be, a WASP—he was, after all, black.

In contrast is the college student who must have served as the role model for this man. He is good looking, an average student and has an exquisite talent for always saying the right thing at the right time. His clothes never look put together but always look right. His girlfriends always seem more like good friends than lovers. *Chums.* He has an outgoing, easy-mannered personality and loves a good party. His sport is crew and his drink is gin and tonic in the evening and Bloody Mary's in the daytime. He has never given much thought to the way he is; he assumes it is all inherited and that his father and grandfather behaved much the same way, which indeed they did. He has gone to all the same private schools as they did and when he graduates he will inherit a seat on the New York Stock Exchange. He doesn't give much thought to what other people's lives might be like outside of his own small circle and is blissfully unaware that his way of life is not the only way of life. From his point of view he is pretty much an ordinary guy; from the outsider's point of view he is not the average White Anglo–Saxon Protestant; there is something about him that only belongs to those commonly referred to as "privileged."

It would not be entirely incorrect to say that our subject matter is those people who consider themselves, or are considered by others, to be privileged, and this group is not confined to White Anglo–Saxon Protestants. Separating the two, however, is not so easy. Historically WASPS have always been well represented in the ranks of the privileged and it has been customary for newer members of this upper tier of society to emulate and adopt WASP habits and lifestyles. We are not referring directly to the majority of middle America when we speak about WASPs, though they may well be subject to the influences of the WASP attitude. These WASPs, who are the ethnic majority of our population, make no special pretense of being WASP; they simply are. It is not ethnicity alone that characterizes the group of individuals who are singled out and labeled WASPs. The distinction is in attitude. It may be difficult to describe, but we recognize it and call it WASP. What we habitually refer to as WASPs are the gatekeepers of White Anglo–Saxon Protestant ethics, an indeterminate population of upper middle- or upper-class people who share a belief system that they cannot entirely consciously acknowledge, for reasons which we hope to make clear. Their impact on all Americans is out of proportion to their numbers in the population. They have established a "norm" for the rest of us to aspire to which has often proved destructive even for them.

The Protestant work ethic together with the British class system is no doubt influential to the WASP way of relating to life. Yet this influence is not just confined to WASPs. It has been influential with every person regardless of ethnic origin who aspires to become an American. If imitation is flattery then it makes sense that WASPs should be full of pride being the progenitors of a national character founded on independence and capitalism. To this extent WASPs set the standard by which the rest of ethnic America judges their degree of assimilation. It is also understandable that especially successful WASP achievers would want to maintain a collective image that is recognizable if they attribute their accomplishments to their faithful adherence to their WASP values.

We realize that to suggest that there is such a thing as a typically WASP personality is to make a broad generalization, and generalizations such as this no doubt pose risks.

However, a potential for a better understanding of behavior *depends* on hypothesis-testing, the riskier the better. By examining what we believe is a culturally conditioned value system we hope that values we hold dear will be more fully acknowledged as an integral part of an *individual*'s personality makeup. Sometimes it is necessary first to unlock the house a person inhabits before it can be possible to unlock the person. This seems particularly true of the WASP, who characteristically only knows himself as the value-structure that houses him. Because of this, understanding the WASP Mystique is to make us conscious of a value system that for too long has been automatically acknowledged by WASPs and those who aspire to become like them as the route to becoming truly American.

ORIGIN OF THE SPECIES

CHAPTER I

The Wasp Character Structure and Its Impact on American Ethics

UNTIL recently it has been considered poor taste or even bigotry to connect certain personality patterns to ethnic origins. Lately, though, there's been a tendency in the opposite direction. There has even sprung up a form of therapy called *ethnotherapy* in which people of similar ethnic origins get together in groups to share the influence, positive and negative, of their backgrounds. Much material exists on the influence of Jewish backgrounds and there are even papers about Jewish mothers and JAPS (Jewish American Princesses). Some papers and books have described the often subtle influences on the children and even grandchildren of holocaust survivors. The focus on Jewish influences was understandable because until recently a very high percentage of therapists and patients have been Jewish. It was only twenty years ago that one of the authors found that nine out of ten of his patients were Jewish. He remembers an incident back then when a patient, a southern WASP in a group of ten, was making some flagrant anti-Semitic remarks. One of the other group members asked her if there was anyone in the room she thought might be Jewish. She looked around. "Well, I suppose only the doctor." In fact, she and the doctor were the only non-Jews in the room.

Well, times have changed and psychotherapy is no longer predominantly concerned with treating the adjustment problems of only minorities. With this gradual change in patient population, psychotherapists and other social scientists have been forced to try to unravel the specific influences of other ethnic backgrounds on personality. Some behavior and value systems become quite mysterious, even incomprehensible, if we haven't solved some of these codes—codes that are often quite unconscious.

Lately there's been an increase in the number of WASPs looking for help in psychotherapy, which has helped in defining and understanding the WASP value system. Again, the WASPs we're talking about come mostly from upper-middle- or upper-class backgrounds—the ones seen in private therapy are also usually restricted to these. To claim a more universal basis for conclusions would be dishonest, although we feel the conclusions mentioned earlier and those to come are valid.

Transcendent for upper-class WASPs is the necessity to

assure themselves of a moral and behavioral superiority, "holier than thou," and to avoid shame and humiliation. Unhappily, this is a position from which they view the rest of the world, which can have especially damaging effects on their relationships with their mates and their families. The unconscious contempt that goes with this often outweighs the human need for less lofty, basic satisfactions in a gratifying relationship. It's a perch that too many of the rest of the population unfortunately aspire to.

When WASPs are in a relationship in which they are the beneficiaries of someone's love, kindness or largesse, they tend to feel uncomfortable and want to change their position. When the situation is changed subjectively, they may continue to enjoy the rewards of a caring friend or mate but in their minds—by some tricky distortions—nevertheless feel they are victims. If the situation is changed objectively they may behave so provocatively they change the caring person's behavior from loving to angry and depriving. Either way, they can be morally superior, even if as victims, rather than recipients of good things from an honest-to-goodness caring individual (who would then presumably be in a position of moral superiority). Being less than morally superior is just untenable—blame it on their ethnic conditioning. For the WASP, it's easier to give than receive.

Some of this can be connected historically to the British attempt to justify their exploitation of groups such as Indians and Africans on the basis of improving the lot of their benighted subjects (Kipling's "White Man's Burden") and seeing themselves as unappreciated victims (as in the movie, "Lives of a Bengal Lancer"). Others like the Spaniards and Portuguese and Dutch and Belgian exploited their subjects outrageously without any pretense of being "good guys." Some further horrible examples of the British choosing "honorable" behavior even over life itself are storied in *The Charge of the Light Brigade* or the battle of Gallipoli. In both instances the British chose to go ahead into certain death in massive numbers rather than to retreat. Death is more acceptable than shame or humiliation. This attitude has permeated our own American society and no doubt had an impact on this country's long involvement in Vietnam, as well as the disasters in Lebanon—we went in to "stand tall" and hundreds of Marines died unprotected. "Death before Dishonor," "Standing tall," "You've had it, pal" often lead our country into impractical and untenable—not to say dangerous—political and military stances. It may sound like a reach, but this is also the message the traditional WASP mother conveys in her admonition to wear clean underwear at all times . . . "You might get hit by a truck and your dirty underwear will be discovered." Humiliation (or somebody's narrow perception of it) is more serious than getting killed.

So for WASPs there is a persistent need to be morally superior. Talk in upper-class WASP families frequently revolves around the "Lady Bountiful" or the kindness of the rich man toward his "inferiors." There is a massive denial of any exploitation of the lower classes. At the same time the

WASP holds those individuals who are the recipients of his largesse in silent contempt. Dependence is humiliating. It takes a good deal of fancy footwork for the WASP to come out as morally superior and even more to come out as victim when objective circumstances indicate otherwise; nevertheless, he or she seems to manage it, often even in relationships to society and also in relationship to those people he or she is closest to: members of the immediate family. WASP parents and children and WASP husbands and wives vie back and forth with each other for the honor of being the greater victim and martyr. It's a contest, a match, and there are a few love sets. Sometimes it becomes too difficult to prove victimization and, thereby, moral superiority. Then comes pressure and guilt from the old superego, and since the superego is "that part of the mind that is soluble in alcohol," this may well account for the high incidence of alcoholism among upper-class WASPs. When objective circumstances indicate otherwise, the second best alternative is to view one's self a victim. And when this fails, alcohol can seem a welcome relief from this unrelenting pressure.

Consider physical love. What is the English way of making love? The French way is oral; the Greek way is anal. The English way involves spankings, strappings and being victimized, shamed and humiliated by punitive authorities such as headmasters or headmistresses. How to explain this? The fantasy punishes the guilty one—often for some very minor or negligible infraction. The person who has the fantasy ends up in the righteous moral position of being the victim of

21

someone's irrational cruelty (rather than its perpetrator). These fantasies of spankings, shame and public humiliation are often eroticized, and though they're also seen in people of other ethnic backgrounds, they seem particularly common to WASPs.

This heavy emphasis on shame and humiliation in WASP discipline is in contrast, for example, to the physical punishment of the Germanic culture. Punishment need not be violent and physical to have a lasting effect on character development. WASPs know that the very worst punishment is being shunned and ostracized—not to be let into the *club,* literally and figuratively. Need of the club is so clearly derivative of the British upper class (any man without a club affiliation is socially unhorsed, not to mention somehow incomplete as a man).

The substitution of contempt and an attitude of moral superiority for an open expression of anger has been taken on as a desirable quality for all Americans, one too many try to take on for themselves. It's perhaps symbolized by the "Ugly American," whose attitude toward the people whose countries he or she visits often is full of condemnation for not being "up to our standards." Good lord, some of "these people" don't even speak English. Imagine *that.*

So elements in the WASP character that have been incorporated into the WASP Mystique are very largely taken from the model of the British upper classes. They involve, among other elements, a heavy emphasis on suppression of overt expression of feelings and an attitude of distance and moral superiority while at the same time maintaining a denial of privilege and a claim of humility and even victimization. Shame and humiliation are to be avoided at all costs. And all of this character has been accepted widely as the norm for Americans who hunger for upward mobility, to be at the top socially. "Just like those damn WASPs."

CHAPTER II

How Did Wasps Get That Way?

IT began with the British—specifically the British upper class. It's of some significance that Britain is now alone among important Western powers maintaining a monarchy. True, the monarchy has little executive or legislative power, it merely gives its royal rubber stamp to the Prime Minister, but the royal family is hugely esteemed by the British, as well as by most Americans. They are exalted as *the* model of manners and behavior, not just by other Royals but by those, there and here, who have nothing like the means to support the lifestyle they hold up as their model. How many young women can afford to sport as many fashionable hats as there are days in the years, as is the custom for Princess Di. England has lords and ladies and dukes and duchesses. There are no such titles in hardly any other major Western country. There's also a sharp demarcation between upper-class Englishmen and middle and lower class. It's clear just by speech patterns to which class an Englishman belongs. For better or worse, the British class system helps them define themselves, gives them models to idealize and idolize and sets limits on their aspirations. More important, for all except the people at the very bottom of the ladder, it provides a measure of self-esteem—after all, there's always a group who's a notch below who can be looked down on.

It was, of course, mostly the English—and lower-class English—who first settled in America. Some of the aristocracy did go South, but they were a small minority. It's not so surprising that having been at or near the bottom of their own social structure, the English settlers now saw an opportunity to set themselves up on top, being the first to get here. The American Revolution in part was a rebellion against the monarchy and the British class system, but ironically for WASPs, who had come here and who had been at the bottom part of the social order, it was also an opportunity to substitute themselves for the old order. American society, ideally aimed to be classless, early on followed the social model of the British class system. The Daughters of the American Revolution and the Colonial Dames, still thriving organizations in our present day society, are testimonials to it. It's an old story: the revolutionaries who overthrow a ruling class quickly set up their own.

Upper-class WASPs in America are broadly a copy of their English counterparts. They copy, or try to copy, their dress, their manners, their tastes, and very important, their sports. And like their English antecedents they try to exclude others who haven't been born into their domains. Except it doesn't entirely work—at least on the surface. "Tennis, anyone?" is the mock cry of those who would share some WASPiness—e.g., the Hollywood-Beverly Hills society. It's possible for an American to climb across the barriers of the *economic* class system and *imitate* the pure WASP, but there's no way to penetrate socially, not really. One can be a guest at the club, but not a full-fledged member. The club stays exclusive, its members and their progeny have a self-perpetuating system of superiority over the "others," and as in England, the "others" have a need to idealize and exalt the unobtainable as a social model that much more to be desired. They look up to the WASP upper classes, try to look and act like them, at the same time knowing that it is all but impossible to enter their hallowed domain. If imitation is the sincerest form of flattery, we tend to flatter to the extent of raising WASPs to the level of an ideal. There are consequences, such as a relative devaluation of other ethnic groups, a dilution of ethnic pride and consciousness—and not just by WASPs, but by ethnics themselves.

Attempts at poking fun at WASPs have always been minor and lacking in any steam. There certainly doesn't appear to be a second social American Revolution fomenting that would knock the people on top off their perch. Quite the opposite. The upper-class WASP styles, clothing and manners seem to be gaining in popularity; ergo, Ralph Lauren's Madison Avenue Polo store, which recently opened to great success. Consider, too, the tremendous publicity that the media gave the British royal wedding of Prince Charles and Lady Diana. For months leading up to the wedding every tabloid and glossy magazine devoted reams of paper to covering every last detail of what went on in the lives of the royal couple. Every day we were told what Lady Di was wearing, how she was styling her hair, how many times she kissed Prince Charles and on and on. We knew when she was angry, when she was misbehaving. We saw pictures of her pouting and pictures of her with captions telling us that she was shockingly inappropriately attired. Rarely were we ever informed of any inappropriate behavior on Charles' part because Prince Charles (unlike his brother) was exemplary of how one should comport himself. He set the standard that his wife-to-be was being measured by. The details of their wedding were not just confined to the gossip columns or the glossaries in supermarket check-out lines. The event and much of the social activity leading up to the event was treated as major *news* even by newspapers that purport to take themselves seriously. What's most remarkable of all is that it was assumed that enough of the American public was so enthralled by the event that they would watch a live broadcast of the wedding and would not be content with a taped version. This meant families were gathered around their television sets at *4:00 A.M.* in order to see the real thing—the royal wedding that had all America in rapture. How to explain this? Just as lower- and middle-class Englishmen want to revere the Royal Family and are even willing to pay heavily for the privilege, Americans who are not upper-class WASPs seem to have the same need.

All of us have fantasies of being very special. Such fantasies usually have no base in reality and most people are embarrassed about their grandiose fantasies if revealed. So we tend to deny our own grandiosity and project it onto some outside person or persons and worship the recipient of these projections. This isn't just an American phenomen, but it does seem that Americans as a group are WASP-worshippers. Who is it, though, whom we are really worshipping? Is it the American WASP, or the British? The American WASPs are surely questionable objects of these worship-like projections, since they are in turn projecting their own grandiose fantasies back onto the royal family whence they sprang.

Feeling grandiose is not sanctioned by the WASP value system. WASPs tend to be predisposed to climb their way to a position of second-in-chief and then to go no further, drawing back their last breath of grandiosity and projecting it onto a sort of deification of Protestant ethics and then submitting to the judgment of an archetypal royal mother. At the moment of judgment there's a sudden fear of success that often holds a WASP back in relation to his non-WASP —and *proud* of it—competitors (compare Ford versus Iacocca), despite his often superior education and early possibilities of achievement. It's his own value system that often prohibits him from gaining or at least enjoying his goal. The WASP who does make it to the top is very often joyless and unconsciously afflicted by his own unknowing guilt.

Preserving a cultural tradition inside a culturally diverse society requires a code of conduct. Mannerisms and behaviors get passed down from generation to generation without being questioned. They end up becoming part of one's personality. Which is why it's said you can often recognize an entrenched WASP at a glance. The behavioral code resonates throughout, is inseparable from personality. If the code were something the WASP could pick up and put down as desired, or expedient, then it could be separated from the WASP as a person. But a WASP doesn't have the same liberty as his WASP-emulating counterparts to put on and take off his fashions depending on whether or not he feels like it. So pity the poor WASP who behaves according to an automatic code of conduct he's rarely aware of and even more rarely questions.

It's not, though, only WASPs who tend to accept this code; it's largely accepted by *all* of American culture as the prototype of tastefulness and well-mannered behavior. So if it has this impact on so many, it's appropriate to look at the origin, meaning and purpose of the code.

At least in part its origins can be found in the Protestant belief in damnation. Both Calvin and Luther believed that God had made an irreversible decision about which of us on Earth had been chosen the "elect." The possibility of purchasing salvation through superior achievements was not sanctioned by Protestantism the way it is by Catholicism. The only way for a Protestant to relieve his fear of damnation was to behave within the strict limits set forth by exemplary biblical figures who were, clearly, the "elect." Living out one's life as a Protestant became a continuous exercise in avoidance of confrontation with that part of oneself that is anything but saintly. To be human is to be damned—which prohibits the Protestant church from acknowledging that the consequences of this doctrine are poignantly human, leaving its followers with an often relentless and deep feeling of unworthiness. To acknowledge this feeling of unworthiness is to come in contact with the fateful truth that one is not a member of that prized group of God's favored children, the "elect."

Good, approved, that is, Protestant behavior is morally irreproachable. One looks out for the other guy before tending to oneself. On the surface it's difficult to criticize this civilized belief-system. Psychotherapy with WASPs highlights a problem. It's the "holier than thou" syndrome, where-in selfishness and selflessness appear to coexist, and not easily. The Protestant faith seems to condition its serious followers to behave in a fashion precisely the opposite of the motive underlying it. The "holier than thou" syndrome is, in analytic terms, a reaction formation, an attempt to eliminate a bad feeling by acting in a way that's the opposite of what that feeling calls for. Fear is eliminated through good deeds. To acknowledge that the underlying motive for altruistic behavior just *might* be fear rather than love is to come face to face with that oldest of Protestant dilemmas—exclusion from the elect. To act out of fear to avoid something is to act selfishly, and to act selfishly for a Protestant is to fall under the curse of damnation.

It follows that it doesn't make any difference what the

underlying motive of Protestantism is when it has been the behavior, not the motives, that have been historically so important to the economic vitality of the United States. Protestant belief is dedicated to building the most civilized of societies. It encourages achievement and growth while disallowing self-seeking and self-aggrandizement, so personal accomplishments are selflessly given up as building blocks of a bigger and better system. If one considers the relative power of the United States, whose roots are planted in Protestant ethics, it's easy to understand why speculating over the true motives underlying these ethics is not a popular pastime and even downright unpatriotic. If it works, why question it.

The American Stock Market is a WASP institution. Since it's part of WASP culture to be versed on the ups and downs of the market, WASPs are generally less likely to lose their shirts than the ordinary man. They are also less likely to spend their money on immediate pleasures than the ordinary man. WASPs tend to be very frugal. When a WASP gets a raise he's likely to invest it in blue-chip stocks for the future of his family and then go home and have three or four stiff drinks while his wife cooks dinner. This is, after all, what his family has done for generations with its money and there's no discussion within the family of other options. The WASP isn't really investing in the future but more trying to defend the lifestyle that his family has grown accustomed to. Money is not meant to be enjoyed but is instead seen as a measure of security (and in some instances divine blessing). As one WASP woman put it when asked if she was wealthy: "The family is comfortable." Delivered in deadpan.

It is a paradox that behaving according to Protestant ethics has often lead to great accumulations of wealth, and yet for WASPs enjoying money for its own sake is not acceptable. For the true WASP, to do this would be self-indulgent and foreclose being able to feel as one of the elect. Maintaining this attitude alongside spates of debutante parties and shooting club expeditions requires some very sophisticated rationalizations.

Since WASPs tend not to display their wealth it most surely isn't money that sets them apart from and above the rest of society. What distinguishes them from other Americans is their unique attitude about *having* money. More and more small fortunes are being made by a diverse group of ethnic Americans, but the WASP domain is still exclusive. Anyone who tries to enter it through the buying power of his wealth risks wondering for the rest of his life why he doesn't quite feel like he really belongs. Attitude, it seems, cannot be bought; it must be inherited. There are, of course, plenty of WASPs who are not especially wealthy but are still recognized and accepted as part of the WASP clan because they were born into it. They may not have had any noteworthy achievements in their lifetime, but this doesn't exclude them from being part of the elite as long as they come from a "good" family.

For WASPs it is not really sanctioned to take pride directly in one's achievements and even less so in the material wealth that may come to represent such achievements. WASPs mostly attribute their accomplishments, as mentioned, to faithful adherence to WASP values—so in a way

33

credit for them is shared by the group. Also, achievement for WASPs isn't nearly as important as affiliation and family background. Never mind displaying material wealth, what counts is being recognizably WASP. Personal accomplishments are a natural by-product of *who* one is.

Plenty of ethnic Americans have proved themselves to be achievers without initially adopting WASP characteristics. They arrive already dedicated to hard work. It's only after they measure their achievements against the potential for further achievement and acceptability, represented most notably in the past by WASPs, that they become at risk to the WASP Mystique. The first thing they often do is change their name to something bland and ethnically unrecognizable. Then perhaps they will move out of the inner city and their association with their ethnic group. If they have the money they may buy their first house in a suburban development where streets have such names as Manor Drive and Chester Court. By the time the next generation has grown up they will be solidly middle-class superficial WASP-like. They will move back into the city to a *non* ethnic neighborhood and buy a small but comparatively luxurious condominium. This generation will have completed college and by the time their own children have grown the thought of maybe sending them to an elite prep school such as Exeter will at least have crossed their mind.

The industrious immigrant is often so anxious to provide the "good life" for his family that from the moment he gets off the boat or plane he never steps outside the path of his goal until he feels he has satisfied it. When he finally does, and allows himself a moment to enjoy the self-esteem he has gained through his achievements, he sees for the first time that he is in a world where nobody recognizes him beyond what his hard-earned dollar can buy. Self-esteem—maybe the most tenuous of all human commodities—seems to make most of us dependent on the approval of others before we can securely enjoy ourselves. Even if he wanted to, the immigrant can't totally avoid assimilation into the WASP culture, a culture that will often reject him no matter how great his accomplishments because socially he is still an outsider by birth and origin.

Since WASPs set the norm and tone in our culture nearly all of America is in competition for their position of superiority. This WASP need to be superior is a value that has pervaded all of American culture. WASPs and non-WASPs who aspire to the WASP standard of behavior too often end up being victims of the values and ideals we've all grown to respect and idealize as being the backbone, the essence of American culture.

Consider, for example, a woman who, about to be left by her husband, badly wants to continue the marriage. When she and her husband got together with a so-called couples-therapist, instead of coming right out with her love and asking him to stay, she persisted in pointing out how he has mistreated and victimized her. What should be a simple negotiation between two people is compromised by the old WASP need to establish and maintain some sort of moral superiority even if it's self-defeating. The wife's always trying to assert her moral superiority is precisely what has caused her husband to want to end the marriage in the first place. Her need to prove herself the morally superior victim outweighs her desire to continue what for her had been a relatively satisfactory relationship. For this woman her marriage is perfectly "satisfactory" so long as she and her husband can compete for a position of moral superiority and altruism. It's her husband, not she, who is unhappy with these terms. He isn't part of the WASP Mystique. But it's destructively at work here.

So understanding the values and ideals of WASPs and the WASP society is to understand better what motivates most Americans to behave as we do, as individuals and perhaps even as a country.

CHAPTER III

The Wasp Value System

RECENT work in psychoanalysis, especially Heinz Kohut's, has focused on self-esteem as determining behavior. In the past psychoanalysts—notably Freud—had emphasized the need for instinctual gratification as the important motivating factor. The English school of psychoanalysts—Bowlby, Winnicott, Guntrip and others—shifted the emphasis to people's need for attachment to other people. It's not surprising that English culture spawned this switch, which reflects typically British character traits. Both the need for instinctual gratification and for attachment to other people have a strong impact on behavior but it's our programming, conditioning, that pretty much decides how we satisfy these needs. How people behave is largely determined by a series of do's and don'ts that is conditioned by what was rewarded and what was punished by parents and our culture or subculture. What were we given points for? What were we given demerits for? If we're given points for conformity and given demerits for iconoclastic behavior, going against the grain, then our ego ideal is especially fixed by this early conditioning.

The pressure on children in WASP families is not, for instance, for achievement as it is in Jewish families. Rather it's toward adjustment and affiliation—in other words, *fitting in*. For a WASP the most horrible sin is being selfish, or seeming to be so, which includes having likes and dislikes and tastes and ideas that are idiosyncratic, strange, unusual. A WASP child is taught the virtue of being seen and not heard, in blending into its upper-class environment and, God forbid, *not* being different. WASPs get their reward for being copies of one another, for suppressing their unique individual feelings and behaving in a predictable group fashion. To stand out, to be *exhibitionistic,* is to break the rules of conformity and invite punishment or public shunning. Certainly sexual feelings, which can often be idiosyncratic, must be suppressed. Similarly anger, exotic tastes in food or clothing, creativity and originality must be suppressed during childhood. If these surface later in adult life they will often be treated as amusements, deliberate eccentricities not to be taken seriously, at worst more to be pitied than scorned. Because of this suppression of creative individuality, WASPs tend to be underrepresented in artistic and creative fields. Among the shortest books ever written must be included "English Music Composers and Creative Fine Artists." Compare the number of Italians, for instance, in these fields. The British and WASP vehicles for self-expression are more in the literary fields, which are less showy, less direct expressions. Actually their writers show a great deal of sensitivity to feelings but they're expressed through characters in books rather than directly, as in music or fine art. If one *is* noticed making a statement, he or she is in danger of humiliation. And the dangers of humiliation far outweigh the rewards of achievement in a creative area. Banking, business and finance are the more unobtrusive areas of achievement, so they're permitted, but the financial rewards in these fields must be underplayed. Or if mentioned, they are best ascribed to the divinity—compare Andrew Carnegie.

Since being a person with a unique self is discouraged and suppression of self and *fitting in* is rewarded, many WASPs grow up to be bland clones of one another. The Self has been an elusive notion in psychoanalysis—so elusive that many analysts have rejected the word as a sort of poetic or romantic idea rather than a practical one. So perhaps it's important to define the term. The Self is a person's subjective view of who he is, how he experiences being in the world and how the person defines his uniqueness and separateness from others. Everyone has this distinction in the mind of others but many lack it in their own minds about themselves. The existentialists probably come closest to this definition of Self when they speak about the experience of being in the world. The Self has a direction, a part that takes charge and tries to make the world as much as possible into what the Self wants it to be. Which is in contrast to the ego, one of whose functions is adaptation to the external world as it already exists. The ego helps people fit in; the Self has an agenda that it wants, sometimes demands, to fulfill.

Without a Self life can be difficult. Without it a person is "other-directed." Since the individual doesn't even *know* who he or she is or wants, there's certainly less chance—close to zero—of being fulfilled. He or she is usually *very* pleasant, doesn't make any waves or give people trouble and tends to be like a chameleon, changing color to adapt to the environment, the situation. This person often ends up being a follower, since others exert the kind of influence that brings about the person's compliance. One such person in group therapy got a standing ovation when for the first time in her life she ran into someone who did *not* like her; it wasn't easy, the experience was even painful, but she was beginning to develop a Self.

How does a person fail to develop a Self? It's simple. If when as infants we're hungry and our mother puts a blanket on us instead of feeding us, we right away begin to distrust our own perceptions. We need to stay connected to our mothers or other significant people around us. If what *we* experience as hatred from mother she calls love, then once again we distrust our perceptions in order to maintain our attachment which, after all, is vital to our physical survival. If the only way to survive with mother or others is to deny our subjective experiences and to adapt to hers, then we're forced to do this. If we're in an environment that mostly doesn't put up with uniqueness, punishes us for being ourselves and rewards us for adapting, then we will indeed gradually give up our Selves. Of course, to *some* degree this is always the price we must pay to become socialized (civilized?).

Countries such as the United States and the U.S.S.R. that need to fit people into a work force tend to diminish uniqueness in their populations. Americans, in contrast to, say, Frenchmen or Italians, seem to include many more people suffering from a loss of a sense of Self. The people treated in psychotherapy who have been the most financially successful and are the "captains of industry" are often the ones with the least sense of Self. They're frequently the ones who have the mid-life crisis. They've achieved everything their *society* has set up for them as desirable goals—money, position, success, respectability—but inside they feel empty, even alienated from themselves. They've adapted almost perfectly to their environment but they feel dissatisfied. They ask: "Is this all there is? What is the reward for all this *good* behavior?"

Two such men in treatment come to mind. They are both WASPs at the top of their fields in very competitive industries. They live in luxury, have apparently stable marriages but feel their life has little meaning. Both always thought they had to succeed to earn their mother's love. So their definition of success was really their mother's. Both had very ambitious mothers and not very successful fathers. They were the designated strong men their mothers lacked. Both were also talented and intelligent and during their school years their mothers reinforced their performances while simultaneously subtly disparaging their fathers' failures. These men were set on a course where success was greatly rewarded and they responded with one success after another, in true Pavlovian fashion. Who *they* were or what their own personal needs were wasn't at issue for them. They were conditioned to put the awareness of their own needs aside. Each had grown up without a self and without awareness of their own uniqueness independent of their mothers.

When they came into treatment they felt they were merely going through the motions of knocking out one success after another. If they had even a slight or temporary failure they felt destroyed. And even when they were succeeding they felt mostly like well-functioning machines. They had no joy in their lives—were waiting around to die. Oh, they weren't actively suicidal—that decision would have expressed more capacity for expressing personal intent than either had. "To be or not to be," the bottom-line existential question, can't very well even be contemplated without a self. Both at various times said they would have welcomed death as a relief from their compulsive striving in a life without meaning or joy, but neither felt he could consider it as a "viable"—pun unintended but maybe significant—alternative, an option, a choice. If there's no self there are no choices—only compulsions to gratify, appease the significant other or others. One of these men actually used to pray every time he was on a plane that it would crash. This would leave his wife and children an enormous sum of money from insurance and free him from his life that seemed to have no purpose except to provide for them. He had transferred his need to satisfy his mother into a need to satisfy his wife and children. Of course neither his wife nor his children got any real pleasure from his "satisfying" them. In fact, his wife pushed him into treatment, feeling his alienation and inability to connect emotionally with her and his children. One of his children was a heroin addict. This man had followed his mother's conditioning to a tee, but there had been no rewards for him on a personal, emotional level other than his repeated "successes" which were more and more empty.

Such emphasis on self-denial keeps many people, but especially WASPs, from developing into truly separate adults. Many WASP men and women have been described as "latency-age" children—this latency period is between the ages of eight and eleven, before puberty. Many WASPs never achieve the emotional level of puberty. They stay good children invested in pleasing parents and their social group rather than in standing out as individuals after having gone through the separation stage from parents and perhaps their values. This dynamic is reinforced by industrialized societies such as America and Russia that, basically, discourage dissidents and encourage conformity.

WASPs, not surprisingly, tend to be attracted to the vigor and expressions of self that are much more encouraged and rewarded in many minority groups. They may have a secret yearning for a similar freedom from parents and the establishment, but their taboos are too strongly ingrained to allow much more than a sort of vicarious enjoyment of this freedom. And since the WASP Mystique, the misguided idealization and emulation of WASPs, has permeated our society, many of our movie stars, politicians and others given approval by our society have presented the same bland, conforming image. Such as a Walter Mondale, a Doris Day, a George Bush might be a few among numerous examples. Contrast these with the likes of Charles de Gaulle, Lech Walesa, Sophia Loren and Edith Piaf, for examples.

Such a rigid value system structuring personality from the earliest age leaves a person especially vulnerable to psychopathology, particularly if the person manages to question the purpose of such values without knowing how to replace them with something better-suited to him or her.

In trying to understand the impact of WASPs and the WASP Mystique, we have made a list of the points and demerits most of them were raised with. These are, of course, generalizations that may have individual exceptions, but we believe that there is a basic truth to them. Other ethnic groups would have very different lists.

On the surface the good points making up the value system would appear to have a very great deal indeed to commend it. What's wrong with apple pie, loving your mother and saluting the flag? In fact, many of the valued points do have a great deal of value. WASPs would certainly appear on the surface to be easy to get along with, they don't make waves. Little wonder that the rest of the people in our country tend to idealize them and try to emulate them. But it's also useful to look at this value system critically. Without needing to deny some of its realistic virtues, we can try to assess how successful WASPs may be in achieving some of their own stated goals, and more important, the consequences for non-WASPs, bemused by the WASP Mystique.

44

The WASP Value System

Points	*Demerits*
Self-sufficiency	Emotionality
Stoicism—"stiff upper lip" in adversity	Grandiosity
	Bad manners
Not showing emotions	Extravagance
Honesty	Overt ambition
Graciousness	Overt sexuality
Respectability	Flaunting newly acquired wealth
Modesty	Being opportunistic
Keeping a low profile	Selfishness
Gentlemanly or ladylike behavior	Cowardice
	Ostentation
Charm	Vulgarity
Courage	Vanity
Humility	Losing control
Responsibility	Disloyalty
Loyalty	Blaming others for personal failure
Self-discipline	
Morality	Irresponsibility with money
Frugality	Cruelty to anyone in a subservient position
Resourcefulness	
Hard work	Cruelty to animals
Perseverance	Being unhygienic
Denial of problems, internal and external	
Optimism	
High threshold of pain	
Fairness	
Manliness	
Respect for one's family	

Pride in family lineage
Love of animals
Love of the outdoors
Liberal religious beliefs
Commitment to public service
Wit and sense of humor
Verbal ability
Being educated in the liberal arts
Athletic ability for both sexes
Physical attractiveness—more
 handsomeness, for both sexes,
 than beauty
Good sportsmanship—being a
 gracious winner as well as a
 good loser
Being of "good cheer"
Having "good" taste

Self-sufficiency. True, the WASP may not be outwardly dependent, demanding, snivelling to be taken care of; that's the good news. But the WASP is simultaneously very much in need of approval by his own system and perceived peers. He or she is the antithesis of an original, autonomous, idiosyncratic person who dares to break certain kinds of inhibiting barriers for new ground. So while he *appears* to be self-sufficient, he is really a very good boy who conforms to the rules of his own subculture. His *image,* however, is a very attractive one, even seductive, that has been held up by our culture as a model for others to follow.

Stoicism. "Stiff upper lip" in adversity is certainly preferable socially and even perhaps personally to falling apart and getting hysterical under stress. The negative side is that it's often achieved by a suppression of feelings, an inability to react in situations in which it would be not only appropriate but highly desirable for the individual. The same, of course, can be said for "Not showing emotions." At times this can also lead to wrenching difficulties in intimate relationships—psychosomatic symptoms like alcoholism, for example. But, again, the *image* appears highly desirable, admirable, and sets an unfortunate standard for others to follow.

Honesty. WASPs are known for their honesty. In fact, one rarely has to worry about a WASP stealing the silver or cheating in a poker game. For one thing the WASPs we are talking about are usually too rich to need to steal. They also are trained very carefully not to cheat on a call on a tennis court or in a card game or on the golf course. All laudable. Gold-star material. Anyone who has played tennis with someone who makes questionable calls in his favor knows how infuriating that can be. Honesty—Abe Lincoln's walking miles to return a penny of overpayment—is part of the idealized American heritage. But if one takes a somewhat broader view of "honesty," then the WASP and his representation can be severely questioned. What, for example, about the "robber barons"? What about the exploitation of the blacks in the South or Orientals in the West? More recently, how about WASP takeovers of corporations or the white-collar cheating on Wall Street? The *image* is one of honesty, but the same man who may go out of his way to return an extra quarter you gave him by mistake may also rob you of millions with a takeover of your corporation or by manipulating the price of a stock you own. Still, Americans have bought the image of the WASP being *honest* and have fit it into the fabric of the WASP Mystique, idealized and emulated, even if, perhaps especially if, the name is Levine or Boesky. You don't have to be WASP to be caught up in the WASP Mystique. Which, of course, is the central point.

Graciousness. A real plus in so many respects. The ability to handle social situations in a manner that puts people at ease has much to commend it. The other side of the coin is that it represents a formula for dealing with people rather than a direct honest response. It's a great deal of form with little substance. Graciousness may help one feel at ease but also go away empty. No emotional exchange. Graciousness that masks emotion, including turmoil, can be like too many tranquilizers. No upset, but not completely alive either. If graciousness becomes a quality that people can choose to use or not to, it becomes a fixed facade that's used in all situations, it creates a persona that hides the real person.

Respectability. Surely an important component of the WASP Mystique much admired by the rest of the population. By its very definition it comprises a group of qualities that are respected by others. But what is respectable in our culture may not be respectable in another. And respectable may in any case mean mostly to be accepted, to go along to get along—which may deny creativity and individuality. It *sounds* good—he's so respectable . . . but plenty can lurk behind the sound and sight, and often does. The WASP Mystique isn't so far removed—at the extreme—from the too frequent litany on TV from the neighbors about the fellow who committed some unspeakable act—such a nice person, so quiet. So respectable . . .

Modesty. A quality that ranks high in America and also in Britain. Interestingly, it doesn't necessarily evoke the same approval in some other parts of the world. And in ours, a lack of it makes one highly controversial—consider the likes of General MacArthur. It's not universally accepted even as a desirable trait. The need to maintain it has the advantage of warding off envy and diminishing competitiveness in other people. An excess of modesty can diminish a person's healthy, effective self-assertion. Self-effacing can efface self. Which adds to an excellent example of how Americans are taken with the WASP Mystique—we hardly ever question the desirability of modesty. We should.

Keeping a low profile is a sort of extension of modesty. It doesn't, though, have quite the same meaning. It suggests, beyond being modest, the need to be near-invisible, to hide too much of one's light under the proverbial barrel. Genteel WASP-like behavior means not only not bragging about money and possessions, it means keeping quiet about one's most distinguishing qualities, too. How many Jews and Italians, for example, tried to keep a low profile at one time or another about their religion and national origins? Why? Because to be themselves was not to live up to or approximate the WASP role model, *to be American* in the supposed best sense. Such suppression of self to be like the rest can be murderous. Consider the case of a New England-bred Jewish man in the midwest who instructed his children that it wasn't necessary "to shout from the housetops" the fact of their Jewishness. He wanted to fit in, to deny his roots. Is not this to murder identity in pursuit of the WASP Mystique?

Gentlemanly or ladylike behavior. On the surface a quality beyond question to be desired. It's even a strength to be *able* to behave like a lady or gentleman when the situation calls for it. But there's an old joke about the man who was looking for a mate who could be a lady in the living room and a whore in the bedroom. Instead he found one who behaved like a lady in the bedroom and a whore in the living room. In other words, there are times and places when it's important *not* to behave like a lady or a gentleman. And if such behavior is fixed rather than an option, it may be too rigid for many situations. WASPs and would-be WASPs too often misbehave by behaving in the bedroom and the reverse in the boardroom and drawing room.

Charm. A quality that certainly involves the real self and the false self. WASPs and upper-class British are especially known and appreciated for their charm—the bon mot, the quick wit, the pun, the turn of phrase, the sense of humor that enlivens charm. One thinks of Noel Coward and Beatrice Lillie. Americans aspire to it or feel badly about the lack of it. An ability to "turn on the charm" can be an asset. It's swell at a party, in a fairly superficial social situation. But it needs to be used selectively. And above all not as a screen to shut out deeper feelings and emotions. Trying to get next to somebody who is forever charming can raise the frustration quotient to intolerable, and make for an impossible relationship. Too much of the WASPish charm can be like a sunblock to anger, passion and other feelings that allow intimacy and closeness and direct communication between two people.

Courage. Everyone everywhere admires it. To be able to face a situation of danger or pain without flinching or retreating is something we'd all like to be able to do. Again, the British hold the copyright with their "stiff upper lip" for God and Country, and so forth. But courage can also lead to foolhardiness and mindless self-sacrifice. Were the British courageous or foolhardy in the charge of the Light Brigade and the battle of Gallipoli? Was America courageous or foolhardy in not withdrawing sooner from Vietnam? Courage based on bravery and conviction is fine. But it can also arise from fear of humiliation and dishonor. So many American movies—cowboy movies, war movies, crime movies—have incorporated to heart and pocketbook the WASP Mystique of the strong, silent courageous man. Are they heroes, or at least sometimes fools? We tend not to question heroism in any form, to accept it as an admirable quality without qualification. Better dead than Red? Better neither one gets lost in this formulation of either-or. It needs objectivity, not a conditioned knee-jerk response. How often have we heard someone referred to as a real s.o.b.—but he sure has guts. Yes, but guts in the context of *what*—being an s.o.b., that's what. Blame WASP Mystique for our failure to consider this sufficiently in making our evaluations.

Humility is modesty deeper and wider, and it poses the same issue, having as it does a central place in the WASP value system. Not all the greats of world history have been humble; indeed, humility could have gotten in the way of their accomplishments. General MacArthur, a WASP, transcended it. Some disapproved of him. But consider Martin Luther, Martin Luther King, Jr., Mohammad Ali, John McEnroe, Jimmy Connors. None is noted for his humility. Like others of these WASP values, humility is accepted by many of us as we seek to emulate the idealization of the WASP, not because of some inherent value.

Responsibility. Surely an eminently desirable quality that's both personally and socially useful. But it can be negative if it's being adhered to in an *inflexible* way that makes it a travesty of itself. Stretched beyond its usefulness and relevance it can lead to compulsiveness, a sort of functional autonomy of motive, response to "duty" over genuine if difficult personal needs or needs of people close to us. Workaholics are a good example of the bad consequences of a sense of responsibility out of context and control. Flexibility and choice have to be mixed in large doses with responsibility or it can lose its value. Once again, blind incorporation of a desirable character trait from an idealized model can often be a destructive process, even if the trait is generally admirable. And the WASP and his values form that idealized model.

Loyalty. A trait that's very much valued in WASPs, especially loyalty to the family and "one's kind." (When it comes to social inferiors it's more noblesse oblige, which translates as patronization.) Once again, loyalty can be a wonderful trait, but it can also be blind. Homage and fealty to outdated rules and systems can devastate by preventing independent thinking and progress. WASPs are steeped—or is it mired?—in tradition. This may be comforting but it can also be stultifying and destructive. Is staying in a marriage or a partnership or a job that is empty and bankrupt being loyal or self-destructive? Is the tendency of most Americans to follow WASP values an attempt to reinforce roots or a rigid, senseless clinging to an outmoded system that celebrates itself as it leeches the inherent vitality not only of WASPs but of those who mistake their ideals and values as the route to being a true American.

Self-discipline. Without it there can be chaos. With too much of it we tend to be stiff, mechanical and uncreative. This is especially true in the arts. If we are too strict, it can make life a joyless straightjacket. A great deal of self-discipline can inhibit one in other emotional, sexual and creative parts of life. And yet this quality too is almost universally idealized as part of WASPs and accepted by many of us as essential to our own self-esteem.

Morality. What is it? How do you define it? When Gary Hart was asked if he had been immoral he said he could not answer the question because its definition varied in different theological systems. The American "theological system" was apparently enough to have him withdraw from seeking the presidency. The important issue is that the moral system of most Americans is pretty much taken over from the Protestant ethic and this very value system we are now discussing. Most Americans—without going through a conscious process of selection—have taken in a value system that has built into it some rather glaring contradictions about morality. The "Holy War" of 1987—in which many leading figures in preaching American morality were exposed as being involved in sexual and financial practices that were a far cry from what they preached—has shaken up many people's ideas about absolutism and rigidity in the concept of morality. The so-called Moral Majority may not be so very moral and may hardly constitute a majority. Just as there is often a rather large gap between the *image* that the WASP presents and the reality of his life and behavior, there may be the same kind of gap between the image our purveyors of morality show and their underbelly.

Frugality. Is this necessarily a desirable quality? Where does frugal end and cheap begin? Is it so bad to live well? Why should one not enjoy the fruits of one's labor to the fullest? Here's an example of how many Americans have taken a WASP character trait and made it automatically into a universal virtue. We make fun of Scotsmen for being cheap, but admire WASPs for being frugal. When one of the authors asked an accountant what should be done with the money, he said, unaccountant-like, "Spend it." The author realized such a corrective was needed to the conditioning of the WASP Mystique about the presumed value of frugality.

Resourcefulness. Finally a quality about which we can be unambivalent. There can hardly be any downside in being able to figure out the best way to cope with or deal with or "maximize" a situation. No problem.

Hard work. Ah. The epitome of the Protestant ethic. This part of the WASP value system has been almost universally accepted in our culture. There was a minor—and not too attractive—deviation for a while with the hippies, but the yuppies are beating it to death. But who says it is written in

stone that the *best* way to go through life is to work *hard?*
Many people in Italy would think this doctrine totally insane.
How strongly has this particular WASP value been incul-
cated in us. In yuppie New York it is not at all unusual for
people in their twenties to spend sixty to eighty hours a week
or even more on their job. Their object is money, money,
money. And often never mind what one does to get it. The
moral question is—hard work for *what?* It's not enough for
its own sake. Besides, "all work and no play makes Jack a dull
boy." Likewise Jill.

Perseverance. Difficult to fault, if it's in pursuit of a particular goal.

Denial of problems—internal and external. Here is a WASP
trait that is widespread but has little to recommend it. The
head-in-the-sand approach to problems obviously doesn't
solve them or make them go away. It often postpones dealing
with them at the best time. WASPs often refuse to look at
problems in their marriage or in their children until tragic
consequences have occurred. One of the most frequently
denied problems is alcoholism or other substance-abuse. This
quality of denial has been adopted by many non-WASPs. To
"put on a happy face" and "smile through your tears" are
considered desirable traits. Little Mary Sunshine and the
bright-eyed, bushy-tailed person are common in our culture
and have at least in part been taken from WASP examples.
For example, the idealization of Doris Day—the screen version as in "Pillow Talk." Her real life as detailed in her book
suggests tears behind the smiles.

Optimism. This trait is not too far from denial. Of course, in general, it's probably better to be optimistic than pessimistic. Certainly more attractive. "The Power of Positive Thinking" comes directly from the WASP tradition via Reverend Norman Vincent Peale. Still, while optimism may have its place, pushing it too far can lead to the same problems that we've described for denial. And at times it can remind one of the face of the boy on Mad Magazine who says, "What, me worry?"

High threshold of pain. If it's actually physiological, so be it. It can also, if self-imposed, lead to avoidance of dealing with a painful situation while there is still the possibility of relieving it in meaningful fashion.

Fairness. Why not idealize it? The problem is the gap between the advertised ideal and the tarnishing reality. How does fairness unalloyed on the personal level coexist with the idea and reality of privilege, entitlement, exploitation of minorities, destructive corporate takeovers and keeping the children "in their place"? The fairness of WASPs too often stops at the water's edge of those who are members of the club. And yet so many Americans who would never even get beyond the gate of the club have bought into the mystique of WASP "fairness."

Manliness for men. Are WASP men manly? That is certainly part of their image. And yet if one asks the women they're attached to about this, they will often complain that the men are cold, detached, unemotional, unaffectionate and asexual. Still, the Robert Redford WASP image is extremely attractive to many non-WASP women and has been set up as a desirable image of masculinity in our society. The strong, cool, silent type is the American ideal. Gerard Depardieu in France and Marcello Mastroianni in Italy hardly are cut out of that mold.

Respect for one's family. The respect that most WASP men have for their wives and mothers is certainly admirable. The respect may not be accompanied by much warmth or affection, but who can knock it? But when we come to the manner of bringing up children, we are dealing with the near-opposite. Children are *taught* respect for their elders, but they in turn are hardly respected. Who *they* are as individuals is mostly ignored. They're put into a mold that fits into the WASP family system. And respect for Mom and Dad can become a bit fatuous, even if celebrated by Mother's Day and Father's Day. Never mind that Mom may be a drunk and Dad deserted us every weekend for his golf game. On a darker level, let's not forget that we're not so many years away from a time when fractious children were considered the Devil's surrogates. Remember *The Bad Seed* and more revealingly, William Golding's *Lord of the Flies?* Today's *Omen* is in a direct line of descent. All of these are out of the WASP environment and culture.

Pride in family lineage. This the WASPs have in spades, no matter what the character of many of the individuals in the family may have been. And strangely enough, since it is *their* family lineage that is exalted while the rest are disparaged, non-WASPs also admire the WASP family lineage and tend too often to put down their own.

Love of animals. Despite W. C. Field's aphorism that "Anybody who hates dogs and children can't be that bad," love of animals is one of the traits that WASPs have taken over from the British upper class. WASPs are often fanatically devoted to their dogs and horses. On the other side of the coin, hunting is very much a WASP activity. Further, household and domesticated animals are often the recipients of affection that WASPs can't or won't show to one another. Wild animals become the target of open hostility suppressed in their intimate relationships. And movies and books about animals and people's love for them, Bambi, Lassie, Dumbo, etc., have become a part of our desirable image, despite W. C. Fields. It's a cloudy portrait.

Love of the outdoors. No ambivalence about this.

Free exercise of religious beliefs and general love of freedom. These were principles on which our country was founded. The quotations on the monuments in Washington are beautiful and stirring. These are perhaps the cream of the WASP contributions to our culture—one reason being that they were truly original. They spoke out against the British tradition, in contrast to so many other WASP beliefs and behaviors that copied it. And perhaps because this tradition is truly WASP *American,* it has generally persisted in WASP homes and in American culture. There have been attempts in our history to limit our freedom, such as during the McCarthy era, but these have at last been beaten back by the strong traditions in our culture.

And yet disparagement of non-Protestant religions often coexists with this tradition. It's the conflict and hypocrisy that's part of the WASP Mystique.

Commitment to public service. This also originated in colonial days when there were small communities and a necessity to put the good of the community above the individual self-interest. Jean Jacques Rousseau called it the "general will." Also there was a relative egalitarian rule with town meetings and a real sense of democracy that fostered the tradition of public service. This commitment is frequently a tradition in WASP families. And though some of it may come from noblesse oblige, it is certainly socially useful and has been incorporated in a positive way by those who would be WASPs and unfortunately disregarded by many others.

Wit and sense of humor. Nice, but at times they can be used to distance people from dealing with real issues. Though there are some WASP comedians and humorists such as Steve Martin, Chevy Chase and the venerable Bob Hope, it's interesting that most of our comics come from Jewish and Black ethnic backgrounds. Have WASPs lost their sense of humor, or stopped being funny? Maybe they take themselves too seriously, and so, therefore, do the rest of us, in thrall to the WASP Mystique.

Verbal ability and eloquence. Englishmen and WASPs have found their major modes of expression with words, in literature rather than in music or art. There are a number of prominent WASP writers such as John Updike and the late John Cheever. Verbal ability includes a large element of form and style in contrast to direct emotional expression, which suits it to the WASP character. Verbal agility and the ability to "turn a phrase" are very much valued by WASPs and by their imitators, and we are not complaining about it here, just trying to explain.

Being well-educated in the liberal arts. This certainly used to be a very important cornerstone of WASP belief. It had great impact on the emphasis in the curriculum of predominantly WASP colleges such as Harvard, Yale and Princeton. Unfortunately there has lately been such a monomania about economics that senior WASPs and their yuppie juniors appear to focus more on finance and economics. A revival of emphasis on the liberal arts is in the offing, though, if Felix Rohatyn of Lazard Freres spreads his viewpoint that MBA's do *not* make for the best in the financial field and he only hires liberal arts graduates.

Athletic ability for both sexes. Our culture has become more and more focused on the advantages of physical fitness. The only sad part is that, if one is born into a WASP family without having athletic ability, it is difficult to maintain self-esteem despite other virtues.

Good sportsmanship. A very admirable trait and one that used to be a characteristic of Americans. Yet recently certain tennis brats and others have seemed to major in poor sportsmanship. Americans seem to have gone from having the reputation of being the best sportsmen to their current one of being among the worst. Compare certain of our tennis players, for example, to the Swedes, whose conduct on and off the court is nearly always exemplary. Could part of the reason for the change be a revolt against the WASP Mystique?

Being of "good cheer." This is one of the characteristics that WASPs have valued and many Americans have imitated. It makes people pleasant and easy to get along with. On the downside it can be a sign of emotional flatness and denial, operating by rote—like the ubiquitous "have-a-good-day."

Having "good" taste—subtle and refined. This is one of those circular situations. Since many Americans have followed WASP traditions, "good" taste is now defined as WASP taste by many. It's another example of the degree to which the WASP Mystique has been accepted by our culture. Other cultures clearly have different definitions of "good" taste—including belching and throwing up, as our anthropologists can attest.

Now to some of the demerits, the no-no's in the WASP value system:

Emotionality. A definite nay-say for WASPs, signifying weakness, instability. The strong, silent man and the ice queen have long been standards in the WASP family, adapted in turn by movies, models, commercials. They have found a consensus from much of our culture as being the preferred and acceptable way to look and act. But being attached to a strong silent man or an ice queen has its deficits. Ask the one who must live with one.

Extravagance. Other cultures have not condemned it—the world would not necessarily be a better place minus the Palace of Versailles, the Palace of the Doges, the Taj Mahal and the Forbidden City. Or even without Malcolm Forbes' eggs and balloons.

Overt ambition. Fighting down this trait is a mixed blessing. It may, in fact, inhibit the ability to maximize potential in whatever arena chosen.

Overt sexuality. Likewise a mixed blessing. It can be pleasant, even exciting, to be around a person of either sex who is able to express his or her sexuality overtly but, one hopes, tastefully. And the suppression of overt sexuality can and does often lead to a more general suppression of it—a definite unmixed non-blessing. WASPs are often described by their mates as lacking in passion. Even though Americans have had sex symbols such as Marilyn Monroe and Clark Gable and Lana Turner, they have been removed, up there on the screen or behind the camera. Untouchable, then. The acceptable way for the "right kind of person" to be has often followed the WASP image of asexuality.

Selfishness. This is a WASP dirty word in the cultural lexicon. The WASP is taught to suppress individual needs and yield to those of the family, his subculture and the larger community. They may have a socializing value, but it can also result in a person without a self—without a sense of who he or she is, deficient in will and motivation. A line needs to be drawn between selfishness and enlightened self-interest. Many WASPs and WASP-followers go so far *not* to be selfish that they lose contact with themselves and thereby lose any chance for enlightened self-interest.

Ostentation. Once again the line for what is ostentation and what is an appropriate display of one's virtues or earned possessions has generally been drawn by WASPs and adopted by much of the culture. But there's a difference between flaunting and being open. The WASP impact is to obliterate *la différence.*

Losing control. Jackie Kennedy's behavior at her husband's funeral is a good example of this inbred trait. But what is wrong with losing control of anger or tears or passion under appropriate circumstances? Being house-broken never to share those feelings can lead in the direction of producing a humanoid rather than a human.

Disloyalty. Remember, our country was started by a group of people disloyal to the British. Is it "loyal" to support a person, a cause, a marriage, even a country that is corrupt or evil? Was it "disloyal" to be against our government's position in Vietnam? Is it disloyal to be against the Contras in Nicaragua? Is it disloyal even to question our leaders and institutions? How many times do we hear well-conditioned people say on television that if the President says so, or the boss, it *must* be right. And if you don't like it why don't you go back to Russia with the rest of these Commies? Credit the WASP Mystique. The WASPs strong views on loyalty have permeated an important part of our culture, but our student rebellions and other attacks on the status quo have demonstrated a diminution of their impact.

Irresponsibility with money. This is an important WASP taboo that is certainly laudable. One reason so many WASPs have accumulated so much money is their being responsible (or is it frugal or cheap?) with money. "A dollar saved is a dollar earned." Also let's not forget the notion of Andrew Carnegie, adopted by many since, that "God gave me my money." Flaunting, diverting to illegal income-tax dodges, financed swindles, "insider" stock-market trading . . . all arise from the WASPish taboo, and so anything becomes better than missing out on a dollar—being thereby "irresponsible with money."

Cruelty to anyone in a subservient position. But how about during the days of slavery? Slavery was a WASP phenomenon in America. Cruelty can be avoided now by a position of patronizing, of contempt, and of avoidance of contact. Such a position has been adopted by numerous upper-class people who aspire to be like WASPs.

Men's taking advantage of women. Following the British model of respecting the Queen, WASP men are supposed to be more respectful of their women than other groups and don't take as obvious advantage of them as other ethnic groups do. Pure mystique. There seem to be more battered wives than ever before, for example.

The WASP value system has, indeed, created a mystique that has had and continues to have seriously unhealthy consequences for WASPs and the rest of us who have been conditioned too long to think theirs is "the better way."

CHAPTER IV

What Are Wasps Like?

SO far we've dealt mostly in terms of groups. Here are a series of individual portraits of WASPs and two WASP marriages taken from clinical interviews. They're intended to show the impact of the rigid value system that adds to what *we're* calling the WASP Mystique.

Don is in his forties, a pillar of society who works as a consumer advocate. He is intelligent and moral and righteous. Don spends his days searching out corruption in the Establishment. His co-workers regard him as a model of honesty and integrity and he is admired for his industry and conscientiousness. Clearly he has chosen to question the values of the Establishment in his choice of work, but he is hardly enlightened about how he can live his own life differently from the prescribed mode. Don is a workaholic and his wife is threatening to leave him. On a personal level he is cut off from his feelings. His wife is complaining that she gets little or no attention from him. Months often go by without him making a move to have sex with her. He also has a great deal of difficulty in flattering her or being affectionate toward her in word or deed. On the other hand he is very helpful around the house, a most dutiful good boy who washes the dishes, does the shopping and helps clean the house. He is also very conscientious about doing the "right" things for his children. He takes them to the zoo, the amusement parks and to baseball games. He says he's able to show them a little more feeling than he's able to show his wife, but it's not very much. His son is in therapy on account of a behavior problem in school.

Don acknowledges that he is "unhappy" and is concerned that he has a drinking problem. He does. Though he does no drinking during the day his time at home in the evenings is usually taken up with martinis before dinner, wine during dinner and brandy after. His wife says that she never sees him totally sober at night and that he is usually hungover in the morning. Don's passions are reserved for his work. He has made a moral commitment to clean up and get rid of the no-good scoundrels who violate the ethics of good business. It infuriates him that more people don't seem to care as much as he does. Sometimes he feels like he is forever bailing out a sinking ship. He knows in his heart that what he believes is morally and ethically correct but feels sometimes like he is killing himself trying to prove it. His wife has often suggested to him that he try and accept the fact that he has undertaken the impossible and to try not to be so hard on himself, but for Don to accept this would be to accept defeat *and* to undermine his *own* moral superiority.

Don comes from an upper-class WASP family in Cleveland. His father was a successful lawyer who worked for a large corporation. Don remembers him as being mercilessly authoritarian. One of his sisters rebelled against his authoritarianism, got heavily involved in drugs and left home. She has remained estranged from the family and doesn't communicate with any of them. Don describes his mother as a martyr who put up with her husband's criticism and confined her role in life to raising her family. Don remembers her as being very compulsive about cleanliness. She was a perfectionist who had no tolerance for moral weakness and self-indulgent behavior. Don was always a good boy who obeyed his mother and avoided his father. He graduated from college with honors, got an MBA from a prestigious university and signed on with a well-known firm of consumer advocates.

Don was very shy with women, very "laid back" sexually, as he put it. His sexual fantasies involved humiliating and tormenting women, not too surprising considering the humiliation he endured from his self-righteous mother; he never, of course, acted out any of them. He married a WASP from a good family when he was in his early twenties, still having had very limited sexual experience and continuing his pattern of relative abstinence after his marriage. Don seems "numbed out," going through the motions of living by being a workaholic. Though he feels it's important to help out people who are being victimized, as he does in his work, he approaches his work with such driven self-righteousness that he's unable to get any pleasure from doing it. He has never considered himself a victim—though his whole life expresses this condition. A WASP victimized by his own mystique.

Allison, thirty years old, was brought up in a wealthy suburb of St. Louis. Her father's family had lived there for generations and was one of the most affluent and socially prominent families in the area. Her mother was the daughter of one of the wealthiest men in the country, who also came from a socially prominent family. Inspite of her wealth, Allison is very parsimonious and obsessed with saving money for her future. She is also compulsively neat, orderly, defenses that have worked fairly well for her in controlling and containing her anxiety. Only when Allison's husband suddenly became ill did she realize for the first time how insecure she was and that there was no way she could manage emotionally without him.

Allison, one of five children, was brought up by nannies. Her mother was involved with herself and paid little attention to her daughter. Allison's father, considered charming and delightful by his peers, worked in his father's giant insurance company. He had a reputation of being everybody's friend. He was not ambitious about his own career and felt it more important to get along with his co-workers in his gentlemanly way. Allison claims he had a hard time adjusting to his wife's fortune and that this was the reason that he became an alcoholic, even though Allison describes her mother as being contemptuous toward her father because he was not the success that his father had been. At the same time her mother enjoyed being able to be the one in control of the family. Allison insists that her father was harmless; that his most outrageous behavior would be occasionally to flirt at cocktail parties. He presumably adored his daughter but never seemed to find time to spend with her. His free time was spent golfing or hunting or partying.

Allison was sent away to a prestigious girls' boarding school and then went to a small women's college in New England. She was not a particularly good student, showed little interest in any intellectual pursuit. Not surprising, since as Allison remembers she was never expected to do well, only to learn to behave in a fashion consonant with her social position. Presumably when she graduated from college she would be mature enough to choose a proper marriage partner, someone who, of course, would provide for her. Allison showed considerable talent in painting but it was never developed. Whenever she showed her artwork to her family it was met with indifference. WASP culture isn't hospitable to the volatile passions of an artist. After college Allison taught nursery school for a year, then married and stopped working.

Allison is a conforming, conservative woman. She appears much younger than her age and has the facade of a frightened little girl. She expects her successful banker husband to provide for her and to make all the important decisions in her life. She spends her days decorating her home and taking care of her cats and dogs. She says that she is uncomfortable around most other women of her generation and that most of her friends are women like herself whose first ambition is pleasing their husband and raising a family. Her life revolves around her husband and she is looking forward to having children, being a mother and a housewife. Allison is a quintessential example of someone who has unquestionly accepted the WASP Mystique to the point where she has closed down all roadways that might ever lead to some form of self-expression. She *belongs,* this WASP bird in a cage.

Bill writes radio and television news. He describes himself as the all-American boy next door. His parents were not wealthy but were considered well-off for the small midwestern town where Bill grew up. Bill says that they were staunch believers in the Protestant work ethic, a philosophy he inherited. Bill is bright and attractive; he worked very hard all through school and managed to get into an Ivy League college, which mattered more to his parents than it did to him. In college, he developed a fairly sophisticated persona as well as his talent for writing. When he graduated he went on to journalism school and moved to New York where he quickly got a job writing for television. He says he has been "incredibly lucky" professionally. He now owns a fine house in an exclusive suburb, where he lives with his wife and son. His wife is a country club tennis star, and he takes great pride in her championship record.

Bill's problem? He is depressed unless he is working. Even when he is relaxing he's always *busy* with crossword puzzles, scrabble. He makes lists of things to do and then follows them meticulously. He feels remote, cut off from his wife and son and is chronically filling his time with busy-work in order to avoid such feelings. He also is forever fixing things around the house, even when they don't need to be fixed. If it ain't broke don't fix it is an injunction Bill can't follow. He says he wishes he could develop his writing, perhaps try some fiction, but every time he tries to sit quietly with himself and think, what floods in are thoughts of how emotionally cut off he is and how inadequate he really feels. He has always been afraid of attempting something he could not accomplish and then feeling humiliated for the failure. For Bill the WASP Protestant work ethic has grown to obsessional proportions. Actually, he's caught in a double-bind; he is so threatened by the possibility of failure that he cannot even indulge his obsession except in the most trivial and ungratifying forms of busy-work. For Bill, the message was conveyed early on that he was inadequate unless he was always working. At the same time, no matter what he did it would never be good enough. So Bill has always played it very safe in every area. He has taken few risks financially, socially, sexually and professionally. His safe life is peaceful, except when he allows his true feelings about it to intrude, God and the WASP Mystique forbid.

Bob, in his sixties, was the epitome of a successful American WASP until he retired and became despondent without his work to define him. He came from a conservative, reasonably but not extremely affluent Philadelphia WASP family. As a boy he was both bright and athletic. During adolescence he was not very interested in girls and spent most of his free time reading history, especially devouring every book he could find on the Civil War. He went to Exeter, and there on to Princeton, where he belonged to one of the more conservative eating clubs. He had a few dates with some "appropriate" girls but did not have any sexual experiences or even any intense romances. When World War II broke out he volunteered for the navy, received a commission as an ensign and rose rapidly to the rank of captain. He served in both the Pacific and the European theaters during World War II, and was decorated for bravery. On his release from the navy and after a year of courtship he married "the girl next door," who like himself came from a socially acceptable Philadelphia WASP family. They had three children. Bob became a lawyer and early in his career ran successfully for the U.S. House of Representatives, where he served for eight years. Later he was chosen to be on the board of one of the country's largest corporations and continued to serve on more corporate boards as he got older—at one point he was on the board of three corporations, a university, a museum and an historical society. Unlike most of his colleagues he was rather liberal politically and grew even more so with age, but he never discussed his political beliefs after he left his seat in Congress. Despite all of Bob's obviously good connections he was a man without any real, close friends; tennis and golf partners was about it. Similarly with his wife and children— always kind, never cruel, but much more involved with his history books and athletics than family. All in all he was a quiet man who made no waves and lived his life with equanimity and grace, until he faced mandatory retirement from his various board positions and sensed the pressure from younger partners in his law firm to move aside. At this point his storybook life fell apart.

Bob has lived a life that most Americans would be proud of; most would consider it an American success story. He's been involved in all the most influential strata of society—politics, the law, the military, cultural institutions. He's an example of somebody who apparently prospered by playing by the rules of the WASP Mystique. And yet he feels empty and lost now. He says he feels like he doesn't exist anymore—which is a description of death. When he gets up in the morning he doesn't know what to do with himself without his old routine to direct him. What he's learning, for the first time, is that he has never known himself, been aware of himself, except through his work and associations. With that structure gone, he can't see any purpose in living. He feels dead, this "successful" WASP. It just doesn't seem fair, living by the rules all these years—or rather, for rules read The WASP Mystique.

In contrast to Bob, Angela was, from a WASP point of view, poorly adjusted. In her middle thirties, she grew up in an affluent suburb in Boston and was raised to be devoutly religious until she was sixteen and her mother died. She says her father was a soft-spoken man who never showed any emotion. Angela saw her role in life as being the female equivalent to a "worker-priest." She became a nurse administrator in the public health service and helped take care of the poor. She enjoyed her work because she felt a sense of freedom being around people who were so different from her. She lived very modestly on her salary and never looked for financial assistance from her affluent father.

Her relationships with men was very difficult. She had trouble expressing any of her feelings yet she frequently got overly involved with sexual partners, enjoying the freedom *they* at least showed in bed—she said it never disturbed her she wasn't able to have an orgasm. Angela had a short marriage to a black man who was charismatic but also humiliated her. He had affairs with other women, demeaned her in front of his friends, accused her of being a "white honky" who really hated blacks. After she divorced him she led a restrictive sex life, though she continuted to have sexual fantasies about being publicly exposed, flogged and humiliated. Eventually she avoided sex altogether; even a television show about infidelity made her terribly anxious. She continued to be a conscientious worker at her job but never aspired to a position of leadership.

What she has achieved is her hidden—from herself—agenda of becoming the morally superior victim—not having a good man to love her or take care of her, expiating her guilt about failure by devoting her life to taking care of the poor, living in a modest fashion, having little money and not allowing herself access to family funds, and being cut off from the pleasures and indulgences otherwise available to her. She presents a "holier than thou" air to her clients and the very few friends she still has.

Angela is an example of the unconscious, destructive effects of the WASP Mystique. Unaware of her agenda, she

74

has tried to identify with the oppressed as a way of doing penance for the hypocrisies in the WASP values she was raised on. To a degree her concerns have been the result of sensitivity, but she's taken it to such an extreme that she sacrifices her own life and happiness, to masochistic abuse as in her marriage, or social isolation. She has managed to put herself in the position of being even worse off than many of the victims she is sympathizing with. Quintessentially WASP, she has established herself as the ultimate, morally righteous victim.

Conformity to the status quo of WASP ethics clearly doesn't guarantee a fulfilled or even reasonably happy life. Why? Blame it on the Mystique, at least in significant part.

But does adherence to WASP values inevitably leave one in a place of isolation, cut off from one's feelings and the capacity for intimacy? Consider this marriage. Robert and Frannie met while they were at Harvard and Wellesley respectively. Robert came from a prominent Boston WASP family and Frannie from an equally prominent one in New York. Robert's father was an officer in a brokerage house, as his father had been. His mother was a low-key not terribly socially active woman who ran the house and brought up the children. Robert's home was a peaceful, orderly one, without any particular drama. His father and mother were very respectful toward one another and similarly so toward their children. Robert was brought up firmly but not harshly and had a sense of integrity and responsibility instilled in him by his parents. He was bright but not very interested in academics. He was very popular, had a wonderful sense of humor and was often sought after as a guest at parties. Robert enjoyed hunting and fishing with his father, learning both sports as a young boy. He had a good relationship with both of his parents and a life relatively free from anxiety, including money problems.

Franny, also from a socially prominent and reasonably wealthy family, lost her father in an auto accident when she was nine. Franny's mother went to work and managed to pull the family through on what was a reduced income. Franny had to go to a public school and then worked her way through Wellesley waiting on tables. She majored in art history and showed some skill as a painter. She did well if not outstandingly in college, was a happy cheerful girl who was very attractive in both appearance and personality.

Robert and Franny met during their senior year of college and fell in love. They felt made for each other and decided to marry shortly after their graduation. A friend of Franny's family paid for the wedding and reception so they had a grand wedding and were the bride and groom of the season. Robert immediately joined his father's brokerage house as soon as he graduated from college. He was an outstanding success, thanks to his social skills. Franny, after a very brief stint as a receptionist at an art gallery, became pregnant and decided to devote herself to being a housewife and mother. She became a gourmet cook and was a big help to Robert as a hostess to his clients.

Franny and Robert seem to be devoted to one another and very happy together. Their relationship is characterized by a great deal of mutual respect. They are as gracious and pleasant to one another as they are with their children and friends. This is what all WASP marriages are *supposed* to be. They function as a team, mutually supportive. They live the rules they grew up learning to respect: a wife and mother should devote herself to the care of her husband and children and to perfecting the art of entertaining, which, in turn, is crucial to the pursuit of social alliances; a husband and father should dutifully provide all possible to help his wife's role succeed smoothly as possible.

If Franny were to decide she wanted to work, the balance of this genuinely happy marriage would need to go through some major readjustments. Or imagine what would happen if Robert suddenly decided that he didn't want to work full-time and signed up to learn how to cook so that *he* could be in charge of the entertaining. That would leave Franny without her job of being the gracious hostess, plus a reduced family income. Plenty of American families have gone and are going through these sorts of changes. Every day one hears or reads about the problems of such changes and the adjustments that must be made. Robert and Franny are fortunate enough to be able to be the best of their WASP norm. They are the happy *exception* to the Mystique—which for them is a reality that works. Those like them are not legion.

WASPs have generally been immune, or at least resistant, to the influences of two major social movements bearing down on their society and the rules that they are supposed to play by. One of these is the psychoanalytic movement, the other is feminism. In the instance of psychoanalysis it is very probably true that WASPs would just as soon keep it well out of the clubhouse, but it is perhaps equally true that many psychoanalysts are themselves responsible for this attitude by idealizing WASPs. Part of the reason for this is that many American psychoanalysts focus on *adjustment,* a view that has inherent in it an acceptance of a norm, and many psychoanalysts operate under the assumption, though perhaps unconsciously, that WASP values *are* the norm. Since WASPs are at the top of the socioeconomic hill it seems to follow that they are in a position of power and therefore unlikely to become victims of their society. It's difficult to take seriously the notion that these people are suffering from a lack of socially adaptive traits and skills. So in the past at least some psychoanalysts have actually excluded WASPs by upholding them as the prototypes of built-in adjustment, reinforcing thereby the WASP Mystique.

As for feminism, it's a movement that benefits the middle and lower classes but has little direct effect on women of the upper classes who don't need to work. Many WASP women are antifeminist, though few will openly admit it. The reason is that feminism threatens the equilibrium, real or theoretical, of the perfect WASP marriage such as Franny and Robert have. Even if Franny never entertained the idea of having a career, the feminist movement would still be a threat to her husband's career, since the pool he's competing in is larger and more competitive than when it was predominantly restricted to the sons of the old-boy network and the graduates of the Ivy League. Also, with women in the white-collar work force, the opportunity for disruptive infidelity materially increases.

It's an irony for the present day—WASP ethics still dictate the social values of our culture at the same time they are increasingly difficult to accept or apply. As ethnic America does infiltrate traditional WASP institutions, more WASPs for the first time are facing an identity crisis they can't fend off with the once absolute insularity of their institutions. WASPs are suffering from overexposure to America's consciousness raising, and it would seem only a matter of time before they will have the anxieties that go along with being a *minority* group having to adapt to a shifting majority. As suggested, the single most influential social change that has affected our values has been the women's movement. With women becoming increasingly visible in respected positions in both the private and public section we're reinterpreting the standards by which we judge the quality of our lives. It's unlikely that even as recently as twenty years ago the people whose cases we have just presented would question, let alone be dissatisfied with, the quality of their lives. So at this juncture in social transition it's useful to look at just what it is about the WASP and his or her values that causes us to want to emulate them if WASPs *themselves* are becoming increasingly disenchanted. When those people who represent the dominant value system of our country start turning up in psychotherapy, the opportunity is at hand to explore behavior and its possible pathology as a product of a malfunctioning value system. An analysis of culturally conditioned values is as necessary to understand behavior as an analysis of an individual's character structure. The WASP value system has historically influenced every American's economic, political and religious orientation and set the standard for our aesthetic and moral attitudes. Whether the WASP way of American life continues to be a strong influence in the future depends on each individual's awareness of its influence and the degree to which he is free to choose whether or not to accept it.

Not surprisingly, when we look for familial root causes, Mother looms large and primal.

CHAPTER V

The Mother Ascendant

THE mother in the WASP family is typically matriarchal rather than maternal. She rarely indulges her own maternal nature except to provide the offspring necessary for the continuity of the family. It's the mother's role that is critical to the maintenance and carrying forward of WASP values within the family. Part of this role is played out by keeping up the *appearance* that it is the husband who maintains the family through his hard work and financial success. In reality the husband tends to be more a facilitator than go-getter, providing his wife with a sound financial base. To put it simply, it's up to the mother to define "how we are seen by the rest of the world." This is critical to the WASP's sense of well-being, which in turn depends more on proper affiliations with proper institutions than level of achievement. Better to have gone to Harvard and gotten the Gentleman C-average than to have gone to a local state university and gotten straight A's. (Compare this with a Jewish mother's hope for her offspring, which includes top institutions *and* top grades.)

The WASPs who came to this country in the seventeenth century brought with them an awareness that they could never be members of the upper class back in Britain, so they set out to recreate the system that had, they felt, rejected them, and from which they in turn could reject others. At the top of this British system was and is a matriarchal royal family, with the Queen as the executive critical parent. The WASP mother takes this figure as her prototype for her own leadership of the family and if she is successful at it she conditions the members of her family to play the complementary roles necessary to satisfy this need. This can only happen if the mother and her husband were both on the receiving end of the same conditioning process from their own matriarchal mothers without ever feeling the need to question it. If a husband were to question his wife's motives then chances are the WASP mystique would be broken, if not the marriage.

The WASP mother will ideally assume the Lockean philosophy that her child comes into the world a tabula rasa. He can therefore be shaped and formed to carry the family into the future. Any behavior arising from his own uniqueness and individual needs are considered to be inherited "weaknesses" to be overcome. The most efficient way to extinguish such needs, or at least repress them, is to ignore them. For a WASP mother, her child's weaknesses are identified by what she has seen in her own life as behavior not socially sanctioned. If, for example, a child is constantly demanding attention, then the child gets broken of this habit early on by not being paid attention to. The technique is usually not punishment but a look or a word to secure conformity. She tries to control her family more through a subtle humiliation than outwardly admitting to disapproval. In this she is different from the Jewish or the Italian mother, though the more assimilated (WASPish, that is) the Jewish or Italian mother becomes, the more she will act like the WASP mother.

If asked, most WASP mothers would no doubt deny modeling their role on the matriarch of the royal family; this long-established archetype is an unconscious ambition to which she tends to strive to defend herself, and maybe her ancestors, from the true motive for their break from the British class system—that *they* couldn't make it there to the top. The American WASP nicely eliminates this conflict by assuming that they *are* the top, which of course they were when they originally arrived here because they had only the American Indian to deal with. Being, as it were, their own royal family, American WASPs developed a keen sense of what sort of defensive measures were necessary to be part of the new royal family. And these defenses were and are first learned in the microcosm of the nuclear family, where the mother plays the role of the queen. Again, it's not conscious role-playing, as one can see from the following remark of a WASP mother when asked if she respected her children:

"Don't be silly," she said. "My children will always be well cared for as long as they respect *me*, not the other way around." This grande-damish sort of attitude can build up tremendous rage in children who can't easily figure out what to do with it. From the outside looking in, the mother looks to be behaving with exemplary poise. The child can be at wits' end and about ready to strangle mother (her royal highness) but, of course, can't because even in the earliest years of infancy he has already been unconsciously bitten by the WASP Mystique—he's dependent on his mother, who's mission in life is to behave for approval.

It's very confusing to grow up feeling some of the things Mark, an actor, remembers from his "privileged" upbringing: "I remember once going to the doctor with my mother. I used to have to get dressed up to go to the doctor—this was one of my mother's rules. My mother always seemed very much in control and I guess I liked that—she always acted like she knew what she was doing and I think I took some pride in being all suited up and going with her to the doctor. When we got to the doctor's office I remember how the doorman tipped his hat and then the secretary took care of us right away and I assumed this was all on account of how we looked. But then when we went in to see the doctor I felt completely ignored. My mother acted as if my illness was *her* illness, and neither she nor the doctor ever once asked me how I felt. The doctor obligingly carried on this way with my mother and I left the office hating him for letting her get away with running my show. What really got to me was that he seemed to respect her, sort of like the doorman tipping his hat. I once had to go to the doctor with a friend and his mother. He had broken his arm playing soccer. I really liked this guy's mother. She was this great big sloppy woman—at least that's how I remember her. I don't think she could have cared less about what other people thought of her. While my friend was in having a cast put on his arm his mother was out in the waiting room with me telling the nurses to bring us some games to play. We sat on the floor of the waiting room with a whole pile of games and books spread out all around us and all I kept thinking was that if my mother were to see me sitting there on the office floor she would have given me a look that could kill. I was really enjoying myself but at the same time I couldn't help being critical of my friend's mother. It was as though part of me was all dressed up in my suit and saying to myself, 'Really, lady, you have no manners.' "

The Mystique grows deep.

Myra grew up thinking her mother was perfect. She had always been involved in charity organizations while at the same time managing to run the family and orchestrate activities so that there was never, well, hardly ever, a wasted minute. This grand illusion was spoiled for Myra, then in her twenties, when her mother told her that she and her brother had ruined for their mother what might have been a promising career as an artist. This devastated Myra, who had patterned her life after her mother, who was so full of selfless propriety. Myra, like Mark, had internalized such a suffocating degree of respect for her mother's propriety, her *rightness,* that her own life was joyless. And rather than recognize the emptiness of her own life and how she might live it differently, she was filled with guilt that her mother couldn't be the artist that she said she had wanted to be. It seemed unfair to her that her mother, whom she described as beautiful and regal, had "wasted" her life.

Eventually and fairly predictably, Myra married a man just like the one who married dear old mom. Her father was a successful banker who was socially amiable but overshadowed by his more charismatic wife. Like her mother, Myra's pretensions exceeded her accomplishments. She was like the wife in "Ordinary People." She had the "right" husband, lived in a beautiful house in the "right" WASP suburb and had the "right" number of children. Her life looked perfect to the outside world, but her inner world was full of real suffering.

Myra was called "Miss Prim and Proper" by her relatively few friends, who observed more than they understood. She was obsessed with correct table manners—never touching the food before the hostess had begun, using the right fork, etc. She never failed to write a "thank you" note. She dressed in tweeds and Laura Ashley dresses. She played down her good looks and good figure, often to the point of appearing quite "Plain Jane." Her rule was never to be noticed, never to be ostentatious. Since everything had to be safe to be perfect, she was unable to capitalize on her skill as a writer. She could also have been called, "Miss Self-Effacing," so adamantly did she hide away any show of success, wealth, attractiveness or talent. This routine of hers certainly avoided any possibility of perceived grandiosity and mitigated any envy she might arouse. It also allowed her to maintain her membership in the "Victim's Association." Myra complained constantly, only in the family, naturally, about being treated badly by her successful lawyer husband and her children. In fact, her husband was a rather passive, amiable man. He was a bit cut off emotionally and, of course, he drank too much. But Myra drank a great deal more. She had three children, all of who provided her with sufficient reason for complaints. One of her sons had been a heroin addict and had just come out of a drug rehabilitation program. A daughter had just had an abortion at age sixteen. The third child had no dramatic problems, but was an underachiever in school. Myra had running spats with them and with her husband. And she blamed all of them for ruining her life. Her despondency over what she called her "bad luck" with her children and spouse led her to drown her sorrows in several martinis every night before dinner, although she did not consider herself an alcoholic. Heaven forfend.

Myra's story epitomizes the state of the broken WASP. It's not just the story of one woman's life. It represents the crumbling of an illusion over three generations. If Myra's children are fortunate enough to recover from their own self-destructiveness, they can avoid the prescription for life set out by Myra and her mother. It's all too often the case, though, that children like Myra's, who are clearly in trouble, carry on a pattern without anybody questioning or even noticing that something might be wrong—after all, they're often at the most prestigious schools and are pushed by their families to engage in the most socially reputable extracurricular activities. The notion seems to be that if the kids are kept busy enough, all will be well and nobody will ever suspect, including the children themselves, that things aren't wonderful on the home front. *Appearances* are what really count to the WASP. So as long as they can keep up the image that their lives are testimony to the perfectibility of the American Dream, they feel they can somehow avoid the realization that as individuals they are often filled with an emptiness. Perfection itself is unreal and thereby empty. The appearance of it is worse.

The passing down over generations of the matriarchal archetype as the idealized mother in this country is a problem not just for WASPs but for the entire American culture so long as ethnic America strives to assimilate what's perceived as a prototypically American character and takes the WASP to represent that, neither understanding nor glimpsing what lies behind the shaky facade.

Freud, some feel, explains this phenomena of the matriarch in terms of penis envy, but rather than argue over whether the matriarchal mother is suffering from penis envy, it would seem more useful to consider what the implications are for all of us if she continues to accept this role and the duties that go with it. Will mother always set the standard for proper behavior by teaching the young the do's and don'ts of the WASP American culture they will have to live in, including the passing down of her own bitterness over the so-called inherent limitations her role as a woman places on her as a person. Consider Myra, who if her children hadn't been so blatantly rebellious would have been quite comfortable thinking that she was living her life the "right" way—every time she picked up a magazine or watched television she would see a reflection of her all-American (WASP-ideal) self. She would conveniently overlook the case of vodka hidden in the closet. For Myra, putting out the image of the "good life" was a self-destructive need, though from her point of view she was just trying to be a good mother. In Mark's case it was a long struggle for him to get over the idea that he preferred the image of his own mother, so unquestionably respectable, over the more indulgent image of his friend's mother. Mark's first wife was typecast after his mother, and his marriage cracked up. Since remarriage his life has been considerably different and better.

What distinguishes the matriarchal mother and her family from the *maternal* mother and family is that the matriarchal maintain their "togetherness" out of fear rather than love. The matriarchal family is—pretty much as it always has been ever since setting foot in America—suffering from a self-centered injury to their self-esteem. The WASP way of life is built on *denying* this injury, which if taken to the extreme can divorce the WASP from his own humanity.

Jews, too, have certainly suffered their own narcissistic injury in their nomadic search for an accepting culture, and it's not unlikely that their outspokenness about their suffering is one of the reasons they have become primary targets of WASP prejudice. But the WASP mother and the Jewish mother share much in common in spite of their different outer trappings. Portnoy's mother and Myra? Yes, indeed. For both mothers guilt is the engine for controlling the families. The difference is in how the guilt is transmitted. For the Jewish mother it tends to be completely out in the open—she wouldn't even *be* a good Jewish mother if she weren't able to provoke some guilt in her family. For the WASP family, they can be hit over the head with guilt and then forever be wondering what hit them because the WASP mother transmits her guilt all unawares and gets the whole family to collude in her scheme. It's very often the case that even after a family's unity is shattered, such as Myra's family's was, the individual members are still inextricably caught up in protecting the family *secret*—the secret, of course, being that they are in big emotional trouble. Because no matter how much emotional trouble the WASP family is in, they will go on denying it until they are blue in the face.

Blue is an unintended pun here—blue for blueblood aspired to, for never saying I'm sorry, for being the regal super-cool ruler, even while the royal house is falling down.

People who value *old* money the most are those who defend old money; unless one confines oneself to this dwindling circle of old-guard WASP families, there's a diminishment in social recognition. So a WASP child raised in the WASP matriarchal family and denied a sense of security is going to have some tough going getting compensation elsewhere. Even if he confines himself to a select coterie that still values his family name it becomes increasingly difficult for him to maintain the comfy insularity he needs to convince himself that there is such a thing as an American class system he has been born into.

To get at this more, we need to go back to the matriarchal structure of the family. The matriarchal mother, as opposed to the maternal mother, has strong narcissistic needs, satisfied best early in life when a loving mother takes pleasure in all the quirky, unique expressions of her child. For the maternal mother doing this for her child comes easily, naturally, and the child starts out his life with a healthy sense of himself, since he's felt it validated by his mother. The matriarchal mother can't give her child this sort of love because she's never been on the receiving end of it herself; she was raised by a matriarchal mother, and tends, like *her* mother, to use her child to give her the gratification she never got as a child. Yet ironically nothing would please this matriarchal mother more than if her children turned out to be carbon copies of herself so that she will have the mirror reflection of herself that she still so badly needs. Instead, her children grow up to be reflections of the values the matriarchal mother took to be herself, and so the vicious cycle goes on. Her children live their lives as if they were protecting their long dead ancestors.

Although the women's movement has been characterized by some of its critics as slighting the role of woman as mother, it has in fact rather accelerated the modification of the woman's role from matriarch to maternal, with its emphasis on the need of the working woman for decent child care facilities, pregnancy and childbirth leave, and other benefits that make it possible for a woman to be a full working citizen and at the same time care for her children in a *maternal* fashion. So the WASP prototype of the matriarchal figure is being modified in our society, but like most social change, it's slow and gradual. The WASP way of securing self-esteem still tends to be more through the "right" affiliations rather than achievement, and so the WASP matriarch survives as a model for the rest of society. She just can't be easily dethroned.

Her way and the way of her children seem from the outside tranquil, under control, unruffled—the gin or vodka bottle is hidden from public view—so why shouldn't the rest of society look to the WASP way as the model to be followed?

But what of the WASP child raised from infancy to suit mother's needs and learning how to behave as mother hopes and makes clear she wants him to behave. Satisfying her is the route to a guarantee of her love. And later he may never realize that his true nature has been absorbed in his mother's values if these same values are reflected in the society that becomes a part of him and that he becomes a part of. The mirror is of mother, which defines self, from infancy to adulthood. Of course this mirror becomes more difficult and elusive as America in fact becomes less WASPish, but it's still largely true that the WASP influence on America and its values is far out of proportion to actual numbers, so one can still easily find validation for the WASP persona from the large number of non-WASPs who are imitating WASPs, or trying to. As for the born-and-bred WASP, this can be unsettling; the true member of the species sees himself becoming a minority in this new culture of WASP look-a-likes, who, of course, will never quite be like him.

Consider Miranda as an example of a WASP who came to the crisis of feeling she had no self—that she was and could only be what her WASP culture defined her to be, with mother setting the pace. For Miranda home felt like an empty fortress. Her family seemed to her to be fiercely trying to defend something without ever stopping to think about what it was that they were guarding, or more importantly, whether it was still worth guarding in the context of the time in which their lives were being lived out. This question was not open to discussion in Miranda's family so eventually Miranda brought her problem into psychotherapy. Even though Miranda was aware of how crippled she felt by the traditions of her family laid down by mother, it was nevertheless a painfully slow process to become free of them.

Attempts to break out of the clinging to traditions, as was the way in Miranda's family, are complicated because, again, when one looks outside of these tight boundaries of WASP traditionalism for some alternate way of life, one finds a popular culture operating on WASP trappings that indicate what Miranda might call the empty fortress is a most prized way of life. Many who do break away from their WASP family roots are stuck out on a limb watching everybody grasp for precisely that which they have struggled to break free of. They become, ironically, outsiders in a culture where they formerly were among the insiders. Sometimes in rebellion they go to the extremes of joining something as antisocial as the Manson Family, or more likely look for a radically different alternative in, say, Eastern religions to break out of the WASP Mystique. But with such breaks, and those far less drastic, can come a feeling of being split between wanting to explore one's own way and wanting to be able to go back home to family for reassurance and unconditional regard.

WASP values—some of them—may have helped civilize us, but as Freud recognized, civilization breeds discontent.

ARISTOCRATS AND PRETENDERS

CHAPTER VI

Some Typical Wasp Habits

TRADITION, or the enshrining of habitual behavior, is essential. Without it the WASP can find himself floundering and frighteningly exposed, with nothing to set him apart from the rest of the population he views as ordinary, to be generous. Since it is critical for WASPs to keep the belief they are the upper class—regardless of economic status—they will often go to great lengths to maintain the traditions they think characterize upper-class behavior. Others not fine-tuned to the ways of a WASP may find some of these habits and behavior anachronistic, quaint and even incomprehensible. But for the WASP certain behaviors are simply inseparable from self.

It is, for example, uncomfortable for WASPs to accept the

egalitarianism of certain public places such as airports, theaters, stadiums, government offices and the like. Having to commingle with the masses tends to bring out their more rigidly defended mannerisms. To particularize, a young WASP woman who traveled to Europe with a non-WASP companion described their trip together as an embarrassment because her companion made absolutely no attempt to hide the fact that he was a "typical American tourist." The rather sad irony of this woman's comment is that her own critical attitude toward her friend made it impossible for her to feel comfortable on their trip together and in the end it was *she* who was the disengaged and voyeuristic tourist. Her friend reportedly had a great time. For WASPs traveling should be no big deal, especially traveling to Europe, which from their point of view is where they really belonged in the first place. They often act as if they were ashamed to be Americans— that original chip on the shoulder from when they first arrived here is still there.

What a WASP may feel to be his or her real identity is particularly noticeable in their traveling habits and views about things European. Look around at an airport. Since traveling tends to unhinge a lot of people, the WASP will guard against this by especially conforming to a WASP identity. He will generally be dressed in his most classic clothes, the older the better. The image he puts forward is conspicuously inconspicuous, neither too dressed up or too dressed down. Real WASPs don't wear jogging suits or the like, even if they are more comfortable than tweeds or shetlands when curling up in a plane seat. A WASP might well find it difficult to curl up in a plane seat anyway, since he has to arrive at his destination looking as unruffled as he was when he started his trip, no matter its length; crossing the Atlantic is to be done with the same reserve and decorum as a short hop from New York to Chicago. Besides, a trip to London is rather less a culture-change than a trip from New York to Chicago. Since the majority of upper-class WASPs are clustered around the cities of the North Atlantic and New England, the boundary of their psychological nationality is perhaps points west of the Philadelphia Mainline but Trans-Atlantic on the east.

Identification with Europe helps account for the WASP having such high regard for things European. There tends to be an assumption that anything European must be better than its American counterpart. There's still a newness about America and its products that WASPs aren't quite sure they want to be associated with. The Americanizing of WASP America is a gradual process, so we have the likes of, say, a Ralph Lauren to ease the transition and at the same time prove that American capitalism is strong enough to exploit its British ancestry.

The WASP who identifies himself with his British ancestry while earning his keep the American way and being free to indulge in all that American society has to offer has either to come to terms with some cultural problems or else resign himself to living a schizoid life. It's not always so easy to have the best of both worlds and come through feeling like a whole person.

A young WASP who as a child was a baseball fanatic

recalls how infuriating it was that his parents would not allow him to go to any of the games because they didn't want him riding the subway, alone or otherwise. They considered baseball the most pedestrian of sports. He was made to feel like there was something wrong with him for loving what he considered to be the ultimate all-American sport. He managed to save two years' allowance to buy himself a tiny portable television on which he watched the ball games in his closet.

A woman who wanted to be an actress despite her parents' disregard for the profession remembers what it used to be like going to the theater with her family. For her the most joyous moment of the evening was when the players took their curtain calls, but this was something that she was never allowed to enjoy because her parents refused to be caught in the crowd when the play ended. They would always leave while the show was still in progress, which embarrassed their daughter greatly. She also felt deprived of the opportunity to share her gratitude for the performance with the rest of the audience. It was humiliating, she felt, to have to follow her parents out of the theater and disrupt the production while it was still in progress—but for her parents it was humiliating to be scrambling for a taxi on the egalitarian terms of a first come, first serve basis. Instead they would take pride in the fact that they had gotten out ahead of the rest of the crowd and this would be often the topic of conversation all the way home, without any mention of how they felt about the play. Shakespeare to the contrary, the play was not the thing—a sense of aloofness from *them* definitely was.

One might say why didn't they have a car and driver? To begin with, it's a myth that most WASPs are wealthy enough to afford such a luxury. And those who are don't indulge in it easily; limousines are not really in keeping with the WASP's image of himself. They cry out for attention, and most WASPs would sooner be dead than admit to this kind of, by their lights, shameless showiness. An acceptable alternative would be to hire the cook's nephew who's on a scholarship at Harvard to drive the family car. This sort of arrangement is ideal because it lets everybody feel as if they are doing each other a favor—that is, until the nephew complains to the cook that her employers didn't tip him. Never mind that it's on account of them (from *their* point of view) that he ended up getting into Harvard; good connections don't pay the rent. The Cook may have a difficult time deciding whose side she's on. She is devoted to her employers but they seem to operate by a special set of rules. The WASP will be equally baffled by the disgruntled youth, because true WASPs can't really come to grips with the *concept* of tipping. Such a conundrum was resolved thusly by one very prominent WASP: he hires a chauffeur and then asks the chauffeur to ride as a passenger while he drives the family car. Only when it's time to park the car does he let the chauffeur take over.

It's revealing that tipping is a difficult custom for WASPs, and would-be WASPs, to accept. From their point of view a *social* exchange has been replaced by an *economic* one. It shouldn't be necessary to offer money to show one's appreciation. A smiling thank you should suffice. Such recognition has its own reward. For many WASPs money and good manners are mutually exclusive—it's a no-no, for example, to talk about one's money—and they resent our culture not allowing them the choice of showing their graciousness the "polite" way. It is much more civilized simply to say "thank you." In the end the WASP will give a tip if he knows that it's expected, but his resentment over being coerced into this position may show itself in the way he leaves his tips.

Having a hard time conveying that he wishes to say thank you at the same time that he is giving somebody money, he may divorce himself from any personal involvement in the situation by sneaking the tip into the recipient's pocket or palm as if the whole transaction is something to be hidden and not quite respectable. Which, of course, tends to leave the recipient feeling guilty rather than appreciative. Tipping in restaurants is somewhat easier but many WASPs resent having to leave this impersonal sort of mandatory gratuity even more than the kind that requires a personal exchange, maybe in part because there's no opportunity for provoking guilt in this kind of tip. WASPs do like to keep a kind of moral inventory of who owes whom what, not in terms of money but in terms of good deeds. This is one of the reasons that WASPs do most of their socializing in clubs rather than public places.

Independence is important to WASPs, but so is protecting the family name. A paradox. More than any other ethnic group WASPs push their family members to become independent of one another. WASP children have traditionally been, if possible, sent off to boarding schools at the age of fourteen or fifteen, or earlier, and rarely return home again except for Christmas. Grandparents are pretty much *non grata* for more than a brief visit. Siblings are often separated on account of career ambitions, which become greater than family pleasures. Indeed, the WASP family is in a way the prototypical contemporary American family, mobilized *and* separated for the sake of attaining personal fulfillment and career goals. But each member in his own independent way is expected to uphold the family name, to behave properly in pursuit of this. It's rare that a child be told how he or she ought to lead his or her life. The children should know it intuitively from having been, in effect, humiliated at some earlier point in life when they perhaps had the audacity to try out the idiosyncrasies of their own true natures.

Communication in WASP families is notoriously poor— not just communication between parents and children but between a husband and wife. Consider the following conversation overheard by one of the authors in a restaurant:

The husband, perhaps a banker and probably a graduate of an Ivy League college, was dressed immaculately in a dark Brooks Brothers' suit with a conservative tie. He was saying, "The seven-ten from Greenwich has been late practically every morning this week."

His wife, a truly classic thirty-year-oldish WASP beauty was saying, "Really, that happened last spring, too."

"I think it was in April, wasn't it?"

"No, I think it was May."

"Yes, I think you're right. It was May."

"It makes me get to work three minutes late every morning."

"Does it?"

"Yes, I've been late every morning this week."

"It's too bad about the way the Penn Central is run."

"Trains are not what they used to be."

"No, they certainly are not."

"The conductors aren't the same class of people that they used to be either."

"No, they used to be polite. They really took some pride in their jobs."

"Not anymore."

"No, it's certainly changed." . . .

A half-hour later the same conversation was still in progress. "The bar on the train is open in the afternoon now."

"Really, when does it open?"

"At four."

"Four?"

"Yes, four."

"You're sure it isn't four-thirty?"

"Yes, I left the office early one day and it opened at four."

"Well, it's good to be able to have a drink on the way home."

And on through the whole meal about the train. No opinions, no feelings, no personal preferences. Just the train.

WASPs tend to talk about facts and things: they don't communicate with one another. They don't convey their feelings even about the things they do talk about, and they will rarely communicate their feelings to one another *about* one another. That latter is another WASP no-no. One can be in the company of WASPs for an endless amount of time without having any idea how they feel about anything—certainly not how they feel about each other or about you. The agenda, to use the vernacular, is to keep the lid on, not to rock the boat, stick to safe topics. The result is safety, but also boredom.

It occurs that this WASP method of discourse is a bit like a good fencing match when a number of people are involved. The conversation will never really touch on anything important but instead will dance around the periphery of any real issues that might lead to substantive conversation. The rule of thumb is that the manner of discourse and its performance are always more important than the content of what is being said. At a WASP dinner party, for example, the purpose of the party is certainly not to eat nor is it to restore ties with friends. Instead it serves the purpose of perpetuating this ritualistic method of social discourse, which, of course, strengthens one's bonds to the class and lets everybody involved feel a little more secure about their status.

The rule of discourse is occasionally breached, and the group will, pretty much inadvertently, penetrate the *content* of what is being said. Once this mistake is discovered the room will suddenly fall silent while each member of the group anxiously tries to disown any personal responsibility for this gaffe. Generally at this point a joke will break the silence of its deadening weight and the "party" will resume. If members of the group are very familiar with one another this process will come about so effortlessly that the breach and momentary digression into substantive conversation will blessedly go practically unnoticed.

The truly WASP dinner party can be a very foreign affair to the newcomer on the scene, as the non-WASP author of this book can attest. First he will have a difficult time working his way into the conversation because there are rarely any breaks at which he might be able to enter with his comments. When he does finally speak he will feel like he is either holding court, because everyone's attention will be turned toward him on account of his awkward manner of breaking into the conversation, or he quite simply will be ignored. If he decides to keep silent and looks forward to the dinner as some consolation, he will go home at the end of the evening disappointed and probably hungry.

WASP food like WASP talk tends to be safely middle-of-the-road, not very exciting. In addition to being bland, it is rarely plentiful. When invited to dinner at the home of a WASP it's a good idea to eat at home before you go out. This is especially true if you are not accustomed to drinking on an empty stomach. Cocktail hour is an important WASP ritual not to be taken lightly. Trying to abstain with something as compromising as, say, a white-wine spritzer is a dead giveaway that you are not a true WASP—not even in spirit.

WASPs have what may be a unique attitude toward food and eating—which is to look upon the act of eating as a necessity of life, nothing more. They prefer to pay as little attention as possible to man's biological needs and bodily functions. A WASP friend once served half a pound of turkey breast to *eight* of us for lunch, which is as much as many of us hearty eaters normally consume in a single sandwich at the corner deli. For her lunch is not something one eats. It's a verb rather than a noun—an activity that only incidentally includes food, and at that only a mouthful or so. The same is only slightly less true of dinner, a ritualized affair during which the food itself must never become the focus of attention.

Which does not mean that WASPs don't care at all about what they eat. On the contrary, there are some rather strict guidelines about what are and are not acceptable foods. WASPs do not want to think that they are in any way susceptible to trendiness or fashion, so they will sometimes rather deliberately avoid serving foods that the rest of the country is raving about. Nothing disturbs a WASP as much as being told that he or she is being chic. As a matter of fact WASPs enjoy being told that they are being terribly unchic. So a WASP might find it perfectly acceptable and on the cutting edge of true fashion, the old and traditional, to serve mutton with mint jelly or chipped beef on toast. For those who can afford a cook, they will have to eat whatever she knows how to prepare, and if the cook has been in the family for a couple of generations she likely is still preparing the same old things that her employers loved as children. If faced with having to prepare a meal, the WASP will more readily resort to cheese and crackers while spending a half hour concocting the perfect Bloody Mary.

Presumably by the time they get to college, the children of such WASPs will at least have learned how to make and consume a Bloody Mary in order to forget about the upheavals they must put up with in order to make it as a WASP inheritor of the faith and manner.

CHAPTER VII

Profile of a Wasp Princess

SHE is twenty-eight. She is five-foot-seven. She has blond hair and blue eyes. Her figure is boyish, not hourglass. Her shoulders are relatively broad. Her breasts are small. Her waist is rather broad. Her buttocks and thighs are ample—not excessive at this point but in danger of being so later. She has a "peaches and cream" complexion that always looks fresh-scrubbed. She has little body or facial hair. What there is, is peach fuzz. Her face is attractive but not outstanding. Her eyes are medium sized, notable for their deep blue color. Her nose is small, thin, with a slight upward tilt. Her lips are relatively thin, not full. She is a pleasant-looking, attractive young lady. She is not a beauty-contest winner, doesn't cause heads to turn as she walks down the street. But even men not stricken by *"shiksa*-madness" would find her attractive. And those who *are* so stricken would find her all but irresistible. (*"Shiksa*-madness" is usually considered to be some Jewish men's beauty ideal, characterized by the blond blue-eyed WASP. Actually this notion of feminine beauty transcends that of Jewish men, and it certainly has spread to men of other minorities. Basically it has been the type that has traditionally won Miss America contests and played movie and stage ingenue roles. Women who have their noses "bobbed" usually do so to try to get them to look like typical WASP noses. And blue contact lenses are a large item.)

In any event, objectively the WASP princess is quite attractive. How she views herself subjectively is quite different. She can't stand her hair. It is too thin, never looks right. Dampness makes it too kinky; dryness makes it too stringy. Whenever she walks by a mirror she looks at it in disgust. Other people have found the perfect hairdresser, but she never does. The ones she goes to always make matters worse rather than better. Wearing it long is inappropriate because she is too old for that. Cutting it short is too masculine. She has literally a closet full of different shampoos and conditioners; none of them seem to help. Her hair is getting darker. She doesn't want to dye her hair. Maybe a few lighter streaks would help. But that is too *ethnic* (for which some might read Jewish). If only she had wonderful hair half the problems in her life could be solved, or on their merry way to a solution.

Her skin? It is *terrible*. She looks good with a tan, but everyone tells her to stay out of the sun. With her fair complexion she will not only get skin cancer but also wrinkles. There are already plenty of them visible now. By the time she is thirty-five she will look like Mrs. *Pruneface*. Her cousin, who has her complexion, didn't stay out of the sun and she looks like *one giant wrinkle*. She buys every new cream that comes out. All they have to do is promise eternal youth and she adds them to her full closet. She knows that dermatologists say they are absolutely useless, but that does not deter her. She dreads the aging process and looks several times a day in any available mirror for the appearance of wrinkles. She feels as if she still has adolescent acne. Especially before her period, her skin breaks out. And also if anything upsets her, she has tons of Clearasil and zinc oxide ointment around to deal with her blemishes. Between her wrinkles and her acne she feels like Gravel Gertie.

Her eyes? She thinks they are too small. Her lips? Too pale and too thin. She also feels her ears are too big and bulging, but at least her hair can cover that up. She's thought about having her ears pinned surgically, but that seemed foolish. And, it's true, everyone has always told her her ears are perfect . . . Her eyes *are* a beautiful blue, but they need enhancing since they're so small. She does not want to use eye shadow or mascara. That's too *obvious*. And you know the sort who do *that*. But she certainly can't even go to the tennis court unless she has fixed her eyes. Not an inconsiderable accomplishment, it takes at least thirty minutes. Between fixing her eyes and her hair, half the day is absolutely shot. No wonder she can never get anything done. And getting the right shade of lipstick to mask those lips that are too thin, that's another problem. The important thing is that the color look natural, can't be too loud or too showy. We'll just have to forget the bump in her nose. People do say it looks okay. A plastic surgeon she once dated said he tried to get his nose jobs to come out looking exactly like her nose. Oh well, a nasal plastic would be out of the question. WASPs just don't get nasal plastics. So she's stuck with her bumpy nose, willy-nilly.

But for all its defects her face isn't really *that* bad. The real disaster is her body. Too bad she is built more like a boy than like a girl. But even that wouldn't be so bad if it weren't a *fat* boy. Okay, her shoulders are too big. She feels as if she looks like one of the guys who plays guard for the football Giants. Well, those are the breaks, can't do anything about that. But those miniature breasts. They have been the *real* bane of her existence. She used to stuff her bra with cotton when she was thirteen. Later she wore falsies. When she started going out with boys she would always be terrified that she would be humiliated if they touched her and found out. She didn't let them come near enough to touch her. With breasts, as with most everything else in the world, it's the appearance that counts. So too with breasts. Later on small breasts became not only okay but *in*. The ideal figure was the model's figure and *they* had no need to wear falsies. Now she did not have to ward off the boys' hands. Or did she? But even though society said it was okay not to have big boobs, it still wasn't okay with her. She still felt inadequate and even at times humiliated. It was better than when she was a teen-ager, true. Some consolation.

But what about those heavy thighs and big bottom? "What heavy thighs and big bottom? They're absolutely perfect," her friends and lovers would say. She knew better. They were just trying to make her feel good. And even if they were minimally acceptable now, they certainly wouldn't be in five years. And her belly stuck out. She would also check *that* daily or twice daily in the mirror. What could she do? She tried aerobics in a class and also at home on a mat jumping around to Jane Fonda's tape. She tried so hard she wrenched her knee and couldn't do it for a month. Then she went to exercise class. She fell off a swing and nearly broke her neck. So now she has a special trainer that comes to her apartment twice a week. It seems to be helping a little. Maybe the belly and the thighs and the arse are a little firmer and less matronly.

But then come the Knobby Knees, the bowed legs and the big ugly feet. "What nonsense," friends and lovers contend, "you have lovely straight legs and not tiny but *perfectly* okay feet." "Well," she says, "that is certainly damning with faint praise." The poor WASP princess cannot believe anything about her body or face is beautiful or even acceptable. Her mother was forever critical of her appearance. She was always told she slouched, and Mumsy *never* said anything about her was beautiful. She still thinks she slouches. Mumsy was always telling her what was *wrong* with her. And Daddy acted as if she didn't even exist—certainly not as an attractive little girl or later as a budding young lady. Now her view of her body combines both of their long-time responses to it.

She is also constantly worried about body odors. Did she

use enough deodorant? Did it wear out? When she goes to the john she always sprays carefully lest she offend anyway. She has a very hard time going to the john when there is any possibility that anyone around—even her boyfriend—might hear the sounds. She always runs the water to cover up any offensive sounds. Where did she get this from? She doesn't know. Except she knows such subjects were never mentioned at home. She never heard either of her parents burp or fart. Nor her college roommates. She always feels sort of dirty or messy. She showers—actually she prefers baths—at least once and sometimes twice a day, but it doesn't get her over the *feeling*. Mumsy and Daddy were super clean and very orderly. She feels as if she is a slob compared to them. Her period is, of course, a disaster. She worries about it coming on unexpectedly and having an "accident." Blood on her dress would be a humiliation she could never live down. And the smell—the smell again. She uses tampons and is very careful, but she worries all the time about offending.

Our WASP princess is really not very happy with her body and its functions. Bodies are not very acceptable and their functions are even less so. They are really *unmentionable* in her home.

Which brings one to sex. Our WASP princess has never had an orgasm. She had never masturbated until she was twenty-three. She wonders why. Perhaps because she never saw Mumsy and Daddy ever act in any sexual way or even be affectionate with one another. And sex or anything remotely smacking of it was never mentioned in the home. Nary an off-color joke or remark. Then with all the talk of the sexual revolution and several learned books which strongly advised the use of both sexual fantasies and vibrators, she has been able, with difficulty, to have an orgasm. She feels very inadequate sexually and she is afraid of being thought lacking by her partners. Her sexual fantasies are usually masochistic ones that deal with her being humiliated, being exposed and spanked in front of an audience, being sold on slave auction blocks, being forced to be the partner of a disreputable man. She is happy she is not a man, because she is certain she would be impotent. The few sexual partners she has been with do not seem to be upset with her inability to achieve orgasm. If they make note of it at all they usually blame themselves despite her protestations that it is not their fault. She is very naive about sex. Since she does not have any powerful desire for sex, she tries to be agreeable and pleasing to her partner.

She did not have much sexual experience in high school. She went to debutante dances and had occasional dates. Sometimes one of the boys would kiss her. She was cold and did not encourage or allow any petting—for one thing out of fear her falsies would be discovered. When she attended one of the "Seven Sisters" colleges, most of the girls seemed to be having intercourse. So in her senior year at age twenty-two she slept with one of the boys who dated her. She felt very little before, during or after the experience—merely saw it as a necessary rite of passage. After that she had several affairs that lasted for a period of months with men who were interested in marriage. She did not really feel she was ready for marriage and eventually the relationships ended. The men were pleasant and she liked them, but she felt no special love or passion for any of them. Currently she is going out with a young man from a good family who is successful in the field of finance after having obtained his MBA at an Ivy League university. She feels no special passion for him either, but he is pleasant and suitable and they get on well together. She is thinking of marrying him since her biological clock is ticking and she assumes—without any strong desire—that it would be appropriate for her to get married and have children. All her friends are doing it. Besides, *not* to do so would be to stand out in a negative way and be labeled an old maid. In her relationships with men she is usually treated very well and very respectfully. She feels entitled to this because she comes from a good family. Her father always respected her mother in every way. She cannot recall him ever so much as asking her to get him a glass of water or a newspaper.

She did reasonably but not exceptionally as a student. She showed a bit of talent singing with the glee club at her girls' boarding school and once had a solo part. She was admitted to one of the Seven Sisters schools in the East and managed a B-average. She studied fairly hard. She majored in art history and specialized in eighteenth-century French painting. On graduation she became a receptionist at an Eastside New York City art gallery. She had a small apartment on the Eastside of Manhattan, which was supported by money from her parents. After two years she became bored with her position at the gallery and worked for Sotheby's, helping in art appraisal and art auctions. She has two or three girl friends she sees, that she met in college. They are friendly but not intimate; she does not really confide in them. But on occasion she goes to lunch or movies or galleries or museum shows with them and has a pleasant time. She feels uncertain about her intellectual ability or creative talent. She does not aspire to go to graduate school or to pursue any profession. She accepts the fact that she will probably get married to her current boyfriend, live in a rather luxurious Eastside apartment, have a house in Connecticut, have children, play some tennis and lead a rather pleasant existence free from any major tension. Her self-esteem and self-image are not very high. She is very self-critical. But she will give the appearance of a tranquil, happy person, especially if she gets married and has children—the seal of approval to bolster her shaky self-concept.

Her perception of herself is very different from the way she is viewed by others, including her WASP boyfriends as well as her subculture and the non-WASP world. They, especially the last, view her not only as extraordinarily attractive, but cool, poised, self-confident, bright, at ease in every situation and completely in charge of her life. That is the *image* she presents. No wonder all the women want to look like and be like what they *think* the WASP princess is. Obviously there are similarities between the WASP princess and the JAP, the Jewish American Princess. But this is precisely because JAPs are trying so hard to emulate WASP princesses. And no wonder so many men—not only those Jews with *"shiksa*-madness"—dream of possessing her.

CHAPTER VIII

Profile of a Wasp Prince

AND now the male side of the coin. The WASP Prince will be the first to tell you he is not a Yuppie. If he looks like a Yuppie that is because Yuppies are trying to look like him. He is a thirty-year-old investment banker and he may work in the firm his grandfather started. He has an MBA degree and was a poli-sci or economics major in college. He probably went to Yale and before that to St. Paul's or Exeter preparatory school. He attended a small, prestigious pre-prep school for boys near his hometown.

He spends his summers and most weekends on a run-down farm he has just bought in a town that probably has an active fox-hunting community. He is also an avid sailor and had to decide between his love for horses and his love for the water when he bought his country house. In the city he lives in a small condominium apartment until he and his fiancée are married. Then he will sell his apartment and buy a larger apartment, preferably on Park Avenue or the east Sixties. His fiancée has been a friend since his college days. They met while spending a semester studying in Rome. They have known each other for nearly a decade and have only just recently discovered that perhaps they could be lovers as well as friends. This realization came about after an evening that they began together as drinking buddies and ended holding hands all the way back to her place.

The Prince is usually seduced by the Princess just as the Princess is usually rescued by the Prince. The Prince is forever finding himself attracted to all the wrong women. Exotic, to him, dark-skinned women set his heart pounding, but he is generally too distracted by their dissimilarity to act on his passions. Instead he turns his attention to the girls he thinks are just like him but is unable to move toward them because he is not really attracted to them. In fact, he feels secretly contemptuous, or even hostile, toward them because they remind him of his own withholding mother. So he waits until they seduce him, which eventually they will because he is a good catch for a Princess of marrying age. He is happy enough to be seduced and to relinquish control of such matters as sexuality and passion, which were never his area of expertise anyway. The WASP Prince *is* socially nimble and expert in almost any situation he finds himself. Great care has been taken to insure that he will behave well in most any situation, but when it comes to sex he tends to be something of a befuddled bumbler. Don Juan he most surely is not. Later on in life he will have learned how to compensate for this underdeveloped side of himself by becoming a masterful teller of truly dirty jokes, none of which will be targeted— with good reason, since there is little that could be said about WASPs that is in any way dirty. The Prince will be happy and greatly relieved if he can find a Princess who is willing and able to take care of initiating whatever sexual relations they infrequently have, and he will be happier still if in addition to this she will listen to his repertoire of dirty jokes.

The WASP Prince is a role that does not always fare well in the transition from youth to middle age. Once the youthful Prince solidifies his identity with WASPs collectively he succumbs to what can only be described as clubhouse behavior. All of a sudden he will want to wear pants with turtles embroidered on them, or perhaps black velvet slippers with foxheads or ducks when he wears his dinner jacket (which incidentally he will never call a *tuxedo*). He will also have acquired a bit of a paunch that he cannot get rid of because he cannot give up his after-office martinis. In spite of his financial success in banking he feels stymied working for the family firm. By the time he is of middle age his wife will have begun treating him as if he were a child again. In many ways this is just what he has become, in relation to her and his own potential. The WASP Prince typically defers to his wife and allows her to control the family. She makes all the decisions in the family that don't involve money. The only time he is not being told what to do by his wife is when he is at work. This often results in his spending long hours at work, despite not really liking his job, or else spending several hours after work consuming drinks to avoid going home and giving in to his wife's predictable routine. The Prince will never confront the Princess with his discontent because he is so accustomed to being controlled by a domineering woman. Which is what his wife has become. Full circle. The Prince is once again role playing a little boy. And taking his masquerades too seriously for his own good. He is not merely dressing up for fun when he puts on the trousers covered with little turtles, he is literally putting on his identity, as if the world might mistake him for nothing but an ordinary fellow if he showed himself without his costume.

His whole life the Prince has been thinking that the good life is his birthright, which ill equips him to deal with the sort of traumas that happen to everybody, Princes included, over the course of a lifetime. The Prince reaches his prime early in life before he has to deal with life's greater misfortunes, like aging and death. One morning he will look at himself and see that he is no longer a blossoming college youth. The mid-life crisis hits the Prince particularly hard because he does not know who to be if he cannot be a Prince. He knows he will never feel like a king as long as he works in the shadow of his ancestors. However, until mid-life approaches, the Prince will be an enviable example of someone who looks always self-assured and impeccably put together. His clothes are basic Brooks Brothers *but* with a personal added touch to distinguish him from the *others*. For instance, he will wear suspenders instead of belts or he will only wear bowties. Occasionally he will have his suits tailored in London but never tell anybody that he does this. He likes to believe that he dresses for himself, not for other people. This attitude will be particularly evident in his choice of shoes and underwear. It is absolutely essential that his shoes be comfortable and sensible while at the same time being of the finest quality. Likewise, his underwear will be boxer shorts. Comfort and modesty also dictate his choice of swimwear. He can usually be spotted as the fellow with the longest and baggiest swim trunks on the beach. The Prince appears outwardly to be modest in his attitude toward his body; actually he has a sort of compensatory tendency to be exhibitionistic. The same fellow who wears swim trunks down to his knees will often be the first in a group to strip down and dare a crowd to join him skinny-dipping. He will also be the last person to put socks on until it is undeniably frigid.

The Prince, unlike the Princess, is not preoccupied with his every physical "flaw." However, he is equally concerned with putting forward his best performance. The difference between the Prince and the Princess is that the Prince's feelings of self-worth depend more on how he behaves than on how he looks. His self-esteem derives from his ability to take command of a group and effortlessly lead it into conversation that engages everyone. As mentioned, he is the ultimate host, attending to everyone smoothly and graciously.

The Prince may have been athletic all his life but he would never consider athletics something to do to get in shape. He enjoys athletics because he enjoys *sportsmanship.* For example, the Prince is particularly drawn to the sport of crew when he is in college. Anyone who has ever trained for crew knows that it is a grueling sport, demanding top condition and stamina, but it is a *gentleman's* sport wherein teamwork is even more critical than strength in producing a winning shell. Perhaps this is a vicarious way of allowing himself to be dependent in a socially acceptable way. After crew he's likely to pursue lacrosse and soccer, less likely to play football and basketball, pedestrian sports.

The *true* WASP Prince is becoming increasingly difficult to detect because there are so many Prince look-a-likes in the yuppie population. One might say that the male Yuppie is to the WASP Prince what the Jewish American Princess is to the WASP Princess. He wants to be unconditionally accepted as an American and the first step that he will take toward accomplishing this will be superficially to WASPize his ethnicity. Most important, he must drop any hint of an accent in his speech. This is as critical for the would-be Prince as the nose bob is for the would-be Princess—WASP society tends to judge men by what they *say* and women by how they *look*. There is, though, one critical difference between the WASP Prince and the non-WASP Yuppie would-be Prince, though superficially it is difficult to detect: the Yuppie will pride himself on his achievements. He wants to be recognized for what he has accomplished because that proves to him that he has transcended his ethnicity. To excel in the American marketplace is taken as a personal accomplishment for the Yuppie, who underneath his WASP persona still associates himself with his ethnic roots.

The WASP Prince, on the other hand, tends to play down his own achievements—he sees himself as the benefactor, rather than the beneficiary, of American opportunity. He invented it. The Yuppie is admittedly upwardly mobile. The WASP Prince assumes that he has long since arrived at the top. He can only look down on, or ignore, those trying to get there.

CHAPTER IX

The Corporate Wasp

HUGH is fifty-two years old. He is the head of advertising for paint products for a large international chemical company. He started working for the company selling paint to hardware stores shortly after graduation from Princeton and resumed his job after his release from the Navy at the end of the Korean War. He had a rapid series of promotions from salesman to supervisor of salesmen to plant manager to advertising executive to head of advertising of paint products during the boom years after the war and subsequently. He is very well liked by both his employers and subordinates. At first his promotions required his uprooting his family and moving to the city in which the corporation required his services. Lately, now that he is close to top management, his position is secure and he is located in the main office. He makes $150,000 per year plus bonuses, stock options and an excellent pension and retirement plan. His present and his future are secure professionally and financially.

Hugh was born in an affluent suburb of New York City. His father was an architect, the head of a successful firm. He grew up in a large house surrounded by several acres of grounds, including a tennis court on the property. His parents retained a cook, a maid and a chauffeur. He spent his summers at Nantucket, where his family had a second home. He was the oldest of three children—two boys and a girl. His father came from a family of New England ministers. Though he had not gone into the ministry, Hugh's father attended an Episcopal church regularly, was abstemious, correct and morally upright. He was also quite cold and austere and had little contact with the children except during weekends and vacation time in the summer, when he would take Hugh sailing with him and instruct him in the sport.

Whereas Hugh's father was remote with his children, he was devoted to his wife and respectful of her. She was bright, attractive, vivacious and a graduate of Bryn Mawr. She was popular in her group and very social. She never pursued any career or work but supervised her home, her children and the help in a matriarchal manner. If asked, she would say she loved her children equally, but in fact she favored Hugh's younger brother, who had been named after her father. Her favoritism toward him aroused a certain amount of low-key jealousy in Hugh's father, which pushed him somewhat closer to Hugh but not to any major degree. So Hugh did not get much affection from either of his parents.

Until sixth grade Hugh and his siblings were educated by private tutors since there were no really acceptable private schools in the neighborhood where Hugh lived. After the sixth grade Hugh went to a country-day school at some distance from his home but was driven there and back by either the chauffeur or by Hugh's mother in the family station wagon.

As a boy Hugh was a fierce competitor, if only a moderately good athlete. This was a cause of distress since success in athletics received such a high premium from his family and friends. His younger brother was an extraordinary athlete. Hugh just did not have the strength or the speed to compete with his brother or with some of his peers. Partly as compensation for this he developed the reputation of being an extremely good sport, so much so that people more skilled than he sought him out. He was gracious both in winning and losing. He was a team player, like a Bill Bradley or a Dave DeBusschere, who always put the good of the team ahead of personal aggrandizement. He never complained about a ruling against him, never lost his temper, never gloated over a victory.

Hugh spent his preparatory-school years at Andover, the all-boys boarding school in New England, where he was only a slightly better than average student. He did not make the varsity teams on his athletic ability so he became the student manager of the baseball, swimming and wrestling teams. He showed a certain talent at writing and spent a good deal of his free time reading—mostly history and mysteries. Like most of his classmates, he had not much to do with girls. He was basically a man's man, felt anxious and insecure with girls. On those occasions when dances or socials were arranged with nearby girls' schools, he did his best to avoid them. When forced to attend he kept to himself or talked to other boys. His sexual feelings were almost completely repressed. He knew that some of the other boys masturbated, but he did not even attempt it.

After Andover he was admitted to Princeton, following in his father's footsteps and those of several others of his family. At Princeton he also followed his pattern at Andover of not being able to make the varsity teams but getting involved by managing them, which at least got him into the circle of athletes and brought him acceptance and respect. He majored in English history and literature and, once again, was an average student. He chose not to have a roommate but was a member of one of the more prestigious and exclusive eating clubs. He continued to sail and play golf and felt fiercely competitive, though was still always the gracious good sport. In his heart of hearts he felt quite forlorn at never being able to be a star athlete, but he never showed his feelings about this. He considered it extremely poor taste for a man ever to show feelings of weakness or vulnerability or need. Those feelings belonged to women.

Still shy with women, the few dates he had in college were friendly rather than romantic and with friends of his sister or sisters of his peers at Princeton. He was not a steady drinker but on occasion would go out and drink with the boys, sometimes having more to drink than he would have liked and feeling the effects the next day. But he never lost control or was *noticeably* high.

By the time he graduated he still had had no sexual experience. He was quite popular with his peers and had established the ground work for continuing life-long acquaintances with four of his classmates, relationships that were friendly but never intimate. He was not in touch with his own vulnerable feelings. And if he had been, he would most certainly never have shared them with his friends.

After graduation Hugh followed the pattern of many of his peers, joining a large corporation in a relatively low-level job. It was assumed by him as well as by the corporation that this was a kind of apprenticeship—that if he showed any talent he would advance up the corporate structure. Hugh's background certainly suited him to this choice of careers. He was a "team player"; he got along extremely well with his peers; he had a good general education but had no particular interest in pursuing a profession like medicine or law. He did extremely well selling paint to retail stores and to other corporations. His customers liked his low-key personality, his attention to detail and never felt patronized by him or put down because of his social position. He shared jokes and stories with them and established friendly relationships within the bounds of business. He received recognition and pay raises for his industry and success in dealing with his clients.

At which point the Korean War broke out. Hugh could

have avoided being drafted by going to graduate school. However, he did not feel that was either the patriotic or the proper course of action. He volunteered for the Navy, partly because of his interest in sailing and navigation and also because the Navy was considered to have a better class of people as officers than the other branches of service. After all, Hugh had been brought up amid a great deal of privilege. Though he would never have admitted it, he felt that his background entitled him to a somewhat more elevated social position than the average. In fact his background *did* help him get into an officers' training school. Here he did extremely well and received a commission as an ensign in the Navy. The Korean War did not offer much opportunity for combat for a naval officer, but Hugh spent two years on ships in the Pacific theater, was rewarded for his service and was discharged as a lieutenant. During his stint he did not go to prostitutes or seek out any other female companionship on his shore leaves. He enjoyed his naval service and saw it almost as an extension of his interest in sailing. He spent much of his free time reading history and developed a special interest in English naval history. Lord Nelson became his particular hero and he devoured any book he could about Nelson's life and career. But there was still a great deal of time to kill with no particular place to go and no special duty. Hugh began drinking somewhat more steadily and in greater quantities than he had before. The alcohol helped him relax, he would say.

When he left the navy he had his old job waiting for him and got back on the career ladder that he had left. Hugh still had had very little contact with his emotions. However, he did feel occasional sexual stirrings, and began masturbating once or twice a week. His fantasies were not exactly noteworthy—meeting a warm attractive woman, developing a relationship with her and making love to her. There were no kinks in his fantasies. He now decided that maybe he should try to make his fantasies come true. Besides, he was now in his middle twenties and it was time for him to think about getting married and having a family.

With this in mind he began dating a friend of his sister. He had seen her around the house so he felt less awkward and shy with her than he would have with a stranger. She was rather plain looking but nonetheless vivacious and sociable, like Hugh's mother, and was able to carry a good share of the emotional and social load in their relationship. They went to dinner and dances and concerts and were engaged after six months. They had minimal pre-marital physical contact—occasionally engaging in necking, but not more than that. They had a big, very social wedding attended by the people in their circle and rented a modest house that they were able to afford on Hugh's salary. Hugh felt very proud of himself for having mastered his shyness with girls and having succeeded in one of the difficult rites of passage—getting married. He felt he had arrived—that this was one of the high points in his life. He not only had gotten married, but married to a lovely woman who was approved of by his parents and his group. He wasn't, though, able to share his feelings either with friends or even with his wife.

Soon after his marriage Hugh's mother contracted cancer

and died within a year's time. Hugh was puzzled by his total lack of emotional reaction to her death. He literally didn't shed a tear. He didn't even experience mourning. He knew he *should* feel something, but wasn't even able to share *this* feeling with his wife. He went through the funeral dutifully helping with the arrangements and being steadfastly at his father's side but with no sense of loss, and pain only about *not* experiencing pain.

Hugh would have two children—a boy and a girl, and felt a sense of pride and inner excitement about his firstborn being a boy but again didn't show this or really share it. His handing out cigars to his colleagues at work or to the men at his golf club was more perfunctory than a show of joy. His wife became very involved with her role as a parent, and Hugh had stirrings of resentment about her somehow slighting him for the children but he never allowed these feelings to come to the surface and certainly never shared them with his wife. However, as the years passed and he never had any role in raising the children he found himself spending almost all his Saturdays and Sundays at the golf course. He would come home after work every evening, have his two martinis before dinner, have a meal with little conversation, say goodnight to the children and then retire to his den to read naval history or occasionally to watch a television program.

His wife gave dinner parties and the couple was invited out by way of reciprocation. Hugh was especially sought after as a dinner guest. He was attractive, sophisticated and urbane. He had a sense of humor and was an excellent raconteur. He and his wife spent their social time exclusively in WASP circles. They literally did not ever spend an evening with anyone from another ethnic group. Hugh was in no way overtly prejudiced. He was too rational to accept any such notion. But he had a certain quiet disdain for other groups. Earlier in his career some of his customers had been Jews. He formed excellent relationships with them. "Uncle Solly" sent expensive Christmas presents to the family even after Hugh had stopped having him as a customer. His children did not even know "Uncle Solly" was Jewish. But then again they never saw him or knew he existed other than when his annual gifts arrived.

Yet in spite of Hugh's success and social desirability he never enjoyed the dinner parties. He still felt shy. He was aware that he had developed a social facade, but he felt acceptance was directly related to this conscious performance. So these evenings were more a chore than a pleasure. Actually he would have preferred to stay home with a good book. His popularity was pleasant but suspect, not connected to himself—whatever *that* was.

Hugh's relationships to his children were, predictably, friendly but formal. Neither his children nor his wife could ever communicate any problem or anxiety or concern to him. Nor could he do this with his wife or his children. He was more aware of his son as a competitor for his wife's attention than as a "chip off the old block." Of course he could never totally acknowledge this—even to himself. At work and at the club he was respected for his honesty, good sportsmanship and integrity, and was well liked by all. He never once had lost his temper and been flustered or upset by poor decisions by his superiors or mistakes by his subordinates. He could not remember an instance of losing control in his adult life. He had never really gotten angry and he had never once cried. If he felt anxious or concerned he never showed it or shared it. His emotions got most deeply expressed in his love of romantic classical music—Beethoven, Brahms, Rachmaninoff and Wagner. He was meticulous about his dress and grooming. His personal effects, his papers, his tax records were always in perfect order. He had a hobby of carpentry, made tables and lamps that weren't especially artistic but were handsome and well made. His tool room—pun intended and not irrelevant—was always in impeccable order.

No one ever saw Hugh laugh raucously—his humor was wry, controlled—cry or lose his temper either at home or on the job. He suppressed his anger via a slight haughtiness and contempt—being above it all. He was the perfect husband if the measure of perfection was showing respect for his wife. He gave himself points for not displaying his feelings, avoiding expressions of pain or need. He never made any waves, any trouble. He was the consummate, quintessential corporate WASP—a team player at work, at home and at play who always seemed to *fit*.

Hugh behaves the way our society has traditionally expected a man to behave. His image is cheerful, bright, industrious, calm, cool, successful in his work, relatively affluent, with a stable, apparently happy marriage and no internal or external *problems*. A pretty facade, indeed. No wonder most men envy the likes of him and use him as a model for how they would like to be. He is a powerful generator of the WASP Mystique.

And Hugh has never once had to question his behavior because it has always been so well supported within his circle. Occasionally he runs into trouble trying to communicate with his wife but he assumes this is on account of the mysterious inherent differences between men and women rather than any shortcoming in himself or his wife. Also, since Hugh gets a great deal of positive support from his corporate environment, he's able to remain quite independent of his wife, which suits him fine because being needy is not something he is accustomed to or easy with.

Hugh's wife, on the other hand, who is a good corporate wife, is emotionally starved in her role of serving a man who can't allow himself to respond to her. She's not aware of this, though—she has been trained to respect the role of the corporate husband without question. He is a hardworking good citizen and without him supporting her she would not have the liberties that she does. As the corporate wife she can't really afford to work because she has an agenda to fulfill that complements her husband's and is a full-time job in itself. She is his and the family's social liaison, which requires her to be available to attend lunches and openings and support benefits and charities. She isn't much influenced by the women's movement because she does not need to work. Indirectly she is influenced by it, though, because it's influencing the corporate environment that her husband belongs to. Hugh feels the direct effects because women are literally moving in on him. A career is now recognized to a certain extent as a trade-off on family life, for both men or women. Hugh and his wife may even occasionally wonder about whether they're missing something. Hugh may, at times, let himself *feel* a need for more contact with his wife.

But more likely, Hugh's values may be so ingrained that he won't realize what's happening or what he's missing, not to mention his wife. For generations to come, the comforts and rewards of the male-dominated corporate world are seriously being questioned in relation to the trade-off they mean in the rewards of a shared family life. With his WASP background Hugh has easily adapted to being a team player and so has been especially good at being able to put his corporation before himself, always to act in behalf of the good of the corporation. Not so in relation to his own family. For the corporate WASP his *corporate* family always comes first, before both himself and his own family. Self-esteem from performing well on the job is, after all, easier than from having a fulfilling personal relationship.

Hugh's social relations being confined to his small circle of friends provides insulation against the changes going on around him. Without awareness of these changes Hugh can stay content with his life just the way it is. This is not a case of waiting for the other shoe to drop. There are no tragedies or abrupt traumas to report about Hugh, the corporate WASP, and his wife. Neither is unhappy, nor is either likely to be so long as they remain selective about who they choose to socialize with, and as long as these people are available to them. But one must question whether Hugh's "comfortable" life is truly enviable, and remind those who would imitate him to beware of the snares and delusions that can await them—to beware, in short, of the WASP Mystique.

CHAPTER X

The Modern Southern Belle Wasp "Expatriate"

THE traditional Southern belle WASP has been represented frequently in our literature—Scarlet and Melanie in *Gone With the Wind*, Blanche as an extreme case in "A Streetcar Named Desire." Blanche was shown to be an empty, superficial, seductive woman whose main role in life was to be a charming, ultrafeminine, psychologically brittle person with almost complete dependence on her man. She was genteel, well-mannered, soft-spoken, focused on maintaining an image with little room for expression or development of individuality. She is by no means an artifact; she exists today.

But what about the post-feminist Southern WASP? What is she like? How has she dealt with trying to integrate her heritage from the past with the new role that has been

proclaimed for her? How, indeed, does one integrate autonomy and dependency, individuality and being a stereotype?
Many women have only been able to make a sincere attempt
at change by getting out of their family and also by leaving
their Southern environment. And even those who have left
by coming to New York, for example, have often found that
"you can take the girl out of the South, but you can't take
the South out of the girl."

Consider Mary Beth. She decided she would have to leave
home and separate from family before she would be able to
be herself, to break out of the regional WASP Mystique. She
felt she was different from the other girls in her hometown,
a medium-sized city in Alabama. She was consistently first in
her class and had a talent in writing. Being a *Southern* WASP
her identity was almost more tied up in being Southern than
in being WASP. Religion was a very important element of
this identification. Mary Beth's family was devoutly Southern Baptist, which meant severe strictures on behavior, especially in the sexual area. Both of her parents were regular
church-goers. There was no way to be in her family without
being a Baptist and a Southerner over and above being a
WASP. When she entered her teens Mary Beth read books
on religion and psychology that made her start doubting her
family's values. There was no one in the family with whom
she could discuss her questioning of dogma; they were all
absolutists. But she had one close girlfriend with whom she
could share her doubts and her feelings. They agreed that the
only way they could establish any independence was to get
into a college in the Northeast. Maybe if it were prestigious

enough they could talk their parents into letting them go.

So they worked very hard in high school and ranked one and two in their class. And thanks to hard work and the fact that Wellesley College wanted to have a class with geographical diversity, they were both admitted. Mary Beth, however, had a very difficult time persuading her parents to allow her to go. She did finally manage it after assuring them she would resist all evil influences. And since she had been such a very good girl for so long she had credibility with her parents. Mary Beth really had been a very good girl—her rebellion had been wholly intellectual. She had been a model of deportment at home as well as at school. She had dated only for the few sanctioned school dances and had chosen a boy who appeared headed for the ministry. Of course if her parents had considered Shakespeare's Cassius, who thought too much, they might have resisted her blandishments.

In any case, being a student at Wellesley was an extremely difficult transition for Mary Beth. She felt very much out of place and inferior to her seemingly more sophisticated Northeastern classmates. She was accustomed to shining as the brightest girl in her class, but not so here. Her grades were better than average but not at the top of the class. She needed another area to bolster her self-esteem in. Not surprisingly she fell back on her Southern belle charm. With her seductiveness, pretense at being empty-headed, deference to men and role as a sex object, she quickly and easily became the most popular woman in her dorm. Men flocked to her at all the mixers that were set up with Harvard and other men's colleges. She had dates on dates. Partly as a rebellion against her family's values and partly to further buck herself up, she started drinking too much and becoming promiscuous sexually.

Of course, her conscience did not take kindly to her behavior. She became guilt-ridden and self-demeaning, which led to more drinking and more sexual adventures—to get outside affirmation from men and some admiration mixed with envy from her women friends. Through hard work and her superior intelligence she was still able to do reasonably well academically, but the vicious circle that encompassed her life was basically self-destructive. On her visits home during the summer and during vacations she reverted back to being the good girl her family expected her to be, which kept family from having a clue about her other life.

Mary Beth managed to graduate and to get a job in New York in an advertising agency as a copywriter (she had majored in English). She made a very conscious and partly successful attempt to extinguish her Southern accent. She got an apartment that she shared with two of her classmates, who furnished a partial curb on her drinking and her promiscuity. She settled into a job and a reasonably good relationship with one man.

But Mary Beth, would-be rebel, still has a tendency to revert back to her Southern WASP stereotype. She is greatly dependent on her man's approval, feels at a loss without him. When there is even a minor difficulty in their relationship or on her job she becomes extremely anxious. She has to fight off a tendency to drink or to revert to promiscuity when her anxiety level rises. When she acts out she is still filled with guilt and remorse and self-loathing. Her conditioning to be an ultrafeminine woman whose essential worth lies in being pleasing and attractive to men comes back into play when she is threatened with a loss of self-esteem. She may have left home geographically, but emotionally—where it counts most—she has not separated from her parents nor from their values.

You might say she is a victim, however well disguised, of a particularly virulent strain of the WASP Mystique, subdivision "Southern Belle."

CHAPTER XI

An Outsider Visits the Wasp Inner Circle

WHAT happens when an Italo-American psychoanalyst (and co-author of *The Wasp Mystique*) is admitted into the rarified atmosphere of an upper upper-class WASP environment for two weeks? His ticket of admission was his relationship to a young lady (already talking like a WASP) who was a member of this elite circle. The families he had lunch and dinner with, whose tennis courts he used, whose clubs he attended, were the sort who measure their net worth in tens and hundreds of millions. Their homes were palatial and surrounded by miles rather than acres of land. He approached his adventure as an anthropologist studying a tribe of exotics in a very foreign land. His objective stance was, no doubt, a defense against his anxieties about not fitting in.

Despite the wealth of the people he visited, their homes were appointed in a most modest, WASPish fashion. The furniture was mostly early American, French and English Provincial. Paintings were mostly of family members, animals and landscapes. Servants were in residence but appropriately unobtrusive. When hostesses escorted him through the house (always at his request) they played it down. "Oh, this room is a mess. I never have gotten around to fixing it up . . . These old chairs are so uncomfortable, I don't know why we keep them . . . This rug hasn't been cleaned for years . . . When our children bring home friends from college I never know whether I'll have room to put them up . . . It's so difficult taking care of an old house like this . . ."

Ah, yes.

Lunch was modest, to put it mildly. "I hope you don't mind having a few leftovers for lunch." Which was exactly what he got—some scraps left over from a roast beef that were cooked over with a few onions, then some fruit for dessert. He inevitably left the table feeling hungry. Dinner was a bit more plentiful and formal. First there were the obligatory martinis. Dress for dinner was jacket and tie for the men, and tailored suits or dresses for the ladies. The ladies' jewelry was usually a single string of pearls and perhaps some simple earrings. Dinners, usually served by a maid, generally started with a clear soup, followed by a thin slice of roast and some nondescript vegetables. A simple salad followed the main course. Dessert was usually a fruit tart or a pudding. Wine, always excellent, was served with dinner. The host, however, invariably criticized the wine. "I'm not sure this is really the best year for this Margaux." The hostess invariably criticized the meat. "This meat is a little tough, isn't it?" After dinner we retired to the living room for brandy or some port and Stilton (British, of course).

Talk was almost entirely about altogether *safe* outside events—the America's Cup, professional tennis, the *weather.* Even talk of politics was avoided. There were few opinions, no expressed feeling about even the safe topics. When people were mentioned they were always presented as well-meaning good people—at worst the victims of sad circumstances. No strong negative opinions or prejudices were even slightly alluded to, which made one wonder if this was for the outsider's benefit. There seemed to be a pleasant, if faintly sanctimonious, air all about. The conversation was like a minuet; everything in balance and under control. There was a sense of unreality. And yet—or perhaps because of this—he felt that he would be judged badly if he did not appear to fit in, so fit in he did. He didn't feel he had a choice. He could not be negative or controversial. It would have been like letting go a loud fart in church. He thought of two movies, *Ordinary People* and *Interiors.* Everything appeared so calm on the outside, then he discovered, as happened in these films, that there was trouble in paradise. One of his hosts turned out to be an alcoholic. One of his hostesses' daughters was a drug addict. Another child in the family had committed suicide.

One really didn't need to be a therapist to have an idea of *why.* All during the visitor's stay he felt enormous discomfort. There was no way he could be himself in this environment. He, who never gave a damn about what anybody thought of him, felt seriously squelched, *put down* and subdued. He felt as if he were in a sensory-deprivation tank where people are put in atmospheres where they have no stimulation to any of their senses and no responses to themselves from the environment. Being cut off like this can be worse than being in prison with sadistic guards. The visitor had been around phony pretentious people, vulgar nasty people, but this environment was different. The sterility, the pretense of normalcy, the emptiness of any honest emotion was deadly. Who could live in this environment and survive?

He began to get an understanding of the *impact* of being brought up in such an environment. He remembered having his empathy reinforced seeing a play about WASPs in which a daughter confesses to her father that she has left her husband and her three children to live in a lesbian relationship. The father says, "Well, that's fine, dear. Please pass the salt."

Being ignored, unacknowledged, never addressed with feeling or allowed to express a feeling is in some ways worse than being physically abused. Which may be why some WASPs go out of their way to feel abused and to experience themselves as martyrs. It's better to feel *something* than nothing at all. It might also explain why their sexual fantasies are often of being humiliated in public. Being noticed in *any* way—even as the object of public humiliation—may be better than being wiped out by being ignored as a person with feelings.

In the sensory-deprivation tank subjects have developed temporary psychosis. Being brought up in such an atmosphere does not necessarily make WASPs psychotic, but to head off that eventuality they must turn off so much of their emotions that they feel detached, alienated from themselves and from each other.

It can be, for all its external trappings and attraction, a kind of living death.

CHAPTER XII

Look British, Think Yiddish

MORE than any other, the ethnic group that has tended to emulate the WASPs are the Jews. Perhaps the fact that many Jews in America are relatively affluent helps explain this. Perhaps more to the point is that Jews are especially sensitive to the need to fit in on account of their history for so long as a people without a country, historic nomads. Why not identify with those who quintessentially do *belong?* Even Jews who are most possessive of their inheritance, are involved in Jewish philanthropies, are Zionists, often aspire to WASP ways and mores. There are also those who either totally hide their ethnic roots and pretend to be WASPs or, while not completely disowning their heritage, are such copies of WASPs as to be almost indistinguishable from them.

Some even become vicious anti-Semites—a pathetic and distasteful tactic to feel accepted among the perceived elite. The domestic Nazi stormtrooper revealed to be Jewish is a particularly extreme and sick example. The already referred to "*shiksa*-madness," the Jewish man's search for the blond blue-eyed WASP as his feminine ideal, is a more benign example.

In his practice the therapist co-author of this work has seen several patients who were wholly or partly Jewish whose family completely denied their origins—sometimes even from the patient—and pretended to be WASP. A pattern of the effect of this masquerade on the patient becomes discernible and is generally traumatic.

"Money was never the real issue," says Robert, a 29-year-old advertising account executive. "My family always had enough money to play the part. My parents seemed desperate for everyone to think that they were WASPs. Actually I don't doubt that they believed they really were WASPs. I grew up thinking that if you lived your life a certain way that eventually it would sink into your skin by some sort of osmosis and you would actually become whatever you were trying to be. Then I hit the real world and found out that WASPs have no mercy on imposters."

Robert found he could not escape his Jewishness when he went to prep school. He remembers his mother counting the number of Jewish names in the graduating classes at each of the prep schools they looked at. He knew which school would make his mother the happiest—the one with the fewest Jews. That was the one he chose to go to. He was terrified of what she would do if he put her in a position of having to confront the family secret . . . perhaps if he were allowed to be around other Jews he might decide that he preferred being Jewish—an eventuality his mother dreaded. Robert had no problem in being accepted as a WASP at the boarding school of choice. He said, "If anyone had suspected I was Jewish they would never have said so many condemning things about Jews. At least I hope they wouldn't have. I wish now I could have spoken up and stood up for myself, but I couldn't. My identity was all wrapped up in needing to hate Jews. I could never admit that what I really hated was myself. So I became a WASP. I don't mean that I pretended to be a WASP; it wasn't that kind of conscious decision. Part of me became WASP in order to survive in that place. That's when the trouble began.

"There was this guy in our class, Harvey, who was Jewish and it was no secret. We were merciless on him when we sat around down in the buttroom and I was probably the most scathing of all. He had this girlfriend, Lucy, who would come up for dances and everyone thought she was really "Jappy." I don't know what makes a woman a JAP except that she was different from the other girls the rest of us hung around with. The only really obvious difference was that she was sexy. And there we were, a bunch of sixteen-year-olds treating this goddess with the most extraordinary contempt. I really felt sorry for Harvey, but at the same time I also was envious of him. I was intensely attracted to Lucy and I started flirting with her. This went on for about a year. It never amounted to more than a fantasy, even though I felt like I was going to die if I didn't get this woman. The fantasy ended when Lucy told me that she thought it was a pity that I was a traitor.

"I attempted suicide after that, though I don't think I really wanted to die. I was just very confused and felt like I was suffocating in this role that I was supposed to play. That was thirteen years ago and I still don't feel like I've fully broken out of it. I don't go out of my way to hide the fact that I'm Jewish anymore, but a lot of times I feel like I'm still a little Jewish kid looking for the approval of a WASP. Sometimes I can fool myself by thinking that by becoming more and more financially secure I can escape this preoccupation, but like I said, money really isn't the issue.

"Eventually I think I'd like to get out of advertising because I think I'm still playing the same role in my choice of career. It's no coincidence that I happen to be very good at dressing up a product and making it look good enough for the public to want to buy it. It's what I've been doing all my life. It won't be easy giving up something that I'm naturally good at, but I need something with a little more integrity."

A forty-year-old man who was bright and attractive and who had been a pioneer in his particular field and headed a successful business came into his session with this special problem. He had invited his family doctor to spend a weekend with him and his wife at their country cottage. The doctor was about his own age and was described by him as being pleasant and low-key. He had come from a small farm town in the Midwest and had a modest practice in Greenwich Village. His problem was that he was preoccupied with what he should do to entertain the doctor over the weekend. Should he show him the "sights"? Should he take him for a drink at a nearby hotel? What he and his wife usually did over the weekend was "hang out," read, go swimming, nothing very special or active and certainly not glamorous. Why was this man so anxious about pleasing his guest? He felt that whoever he was would not be good enough, that he needed a facade to hide an unacceptable self. He ran through the possibilities that might have made him uncomfortable. Was it because his friend was a doctor? No. Was he wealthy? No. Was he more successful or better looking? No. So what was his guest's edge that made him better and left this man feeling not good enough unless he presented a false self? He answered, "He's a WASP."

This man had two Jewish parents who had both changed their names and basically denied being Jewish. They did not lie to him about being Jewish but they lied to the rest of the world. They lived in a very upper-class WASP community and had sent their son to a very very WASP boarding school where he was the only Jew. He had attended the local Episcopal church and every week he would go to Sunday school. He always felt like an imposter, hiding an identity that was clearly not thought by his parents to be acceptable. All through his life he had felt that he was not good enough. He heard none of the "Jews are God's chosen people" or "we are smarter and more moral than anyone else." He received only the negative message. He felt all right when he was with another Jew, an Italian, a Black but not when he was with a WASP. With a WASP he had to do something special to win approval. His parents' self-hatred had been directed against him and he took it into his own concept of himself.

Building one's self-esteem through one's ethnic affiliation may or may not be the only or even best way, but denying it is surely a form of self-destruction.

A woman in her mid-thirties had a WASP mother and a Jewish father. The father not only totally disowned his ethnic origin but was an open anti-Semite. Both mother and father indulged in anti-Semitic remarks in the home. They lived in a WASP neighborhood and belonged to WASP clubs. The patient's father's name was an ambiguous one, but it *might* have been Jewish. She was occasionally teased for being Jewish but this was a source of good-humored ribbing since neither she nor her friends *really* believed it . . . how, after all, could she be Jewish with two anti-Semitic parents? Which, of course, was the effect the parents intended— achieving a WASP affiliation through their anti-Semitism.

Gradually as she became a pre-teenager she began to notice that her paternal grandmother was, indeed, prototypically Jewish: she had a marked accent and in no way disguised her ethnic origins. The patient understandably became confused . . . she too had become an anti-Semite; if Jews were so bad and her parents had even disowned her paternal grandmother then how could *she* be okay? She began to feel like an imposter; which, in fact, she and her parents *had* been. She went from belonging to feeling like a misfit, a pariah, and now had little to do with boys or girls her age. She excelled in tennis and spent most of her adolescence improving her athletic skills rather than socializing. A tennis racket had no ethnicity. In athletics it was skill that counted rather than where you came from. She got some boost from winning junior championship tourneys.

When she became eighteen she also became very attractive and was chased after by men. She still felt though, inferior to her WASP boyfriends. But—or more likely because of this—when one of them actually proposed she quickly accepted. What's better than being accepted by one of your so-called betters? Given its shaky base, added to by the young man's singular immaturity, the marriage failed after a year. Throughout her adult life the patient always felt not good enough in any circle in which she was not clearly socially or educationally superior. When she dated WASPs she spent hours on her hair and her dress and despite this effort never felt up to par. How could she, being the object of her mother's and father's *as well as her own* discrimination? She was always on the edge of shame and humiliation.

Her secret was now out of the closet, but keeping it there for so long had withered her self-esteem, what she thought of herself. She had always had to prove her right to be in a club that would have refused her admission had her origins been known. And her parents had totally accepted the WASP Mystique—the idea that the only way to be acceptable is to be WASP. It took a very difficult and prolonged analytic effort to reverse the hurtful, negative way she saw herself.

Jane, on the other hand, knew from the beginning that she was Jewish, but it was a secret kept inside the family. Her father changed his name to a French-sounding one and claimed he was descended from a French grandfather and WASPs from Oklahoma. All through Jane's childhood and adolescence she felt like an imposter and she knew why. She went to a school in which she was one of the few Jews, but of course no one in the school knew this but herself. Despite being attractive and intelligent she did poorly in school and was reclusive. She *felt* ugly and stupid. She felt like a mental and physical defective. Being Jewish was something shameful and humiliating—otherwise why hide it?—she inevitably thought of herself as a pariah. There was surely no talk in *her* family about Jews being "the chosen people." Yet as she came into adolescence her beauty was so outstanding that she, also inevitably, began to get positive attention and a rush from the boys in her class. In fact, she was voted the most beautiful girl in her senior class. She was aware of this but it had little impact on the way *she* felt about herself. She still focused on what she perceived as awful flaws in her face and body, and barely managed to get through school.

Feeling as she did about herself, she couldn't have a decent relationship with the WASP boys in her class. Eventually, at age twenty, she married a successful Jew who treated her precisely as her self-image dictated. He disparaged her intellect, ridiculed any attempt she made to use her mind and treated her as a sex object in a sado-masochistic sexual relationship.

In her late thirties, filled with self-loathing and miserable in her marriage, she came into therapy. Over the course of the next five years she was able to get at the roots of her difficulties. She quickly left her husband and had relationships with three attractive, successful WASPs. The reality of them helped overcome or serve as an antidote to the Mystique. Starting as a receptionist because of her total absence of experience, she rose rapidly to be an editor of a prominent publishing house. Her view of herself improved by light years. Her having been told she was no good because she was Jewish and that the only acceptable ethnicity was WASP— along with other negatives in her family relationships—had almost destroyed this bright, talented, attractive woman.

Jack was brought up in a small town near a big city in Kansas. His mother and father both "pretended" to the world and to him that they were not Jewish. Like Jane he grew up thinking he was a WASP just like everyone else in his community. Unlike her, there was no big revelation of the truth, but his parents' pretense somehow had an impact on him by osmosis. Intelligent and attractive, he felt small and ugly and weak. He did well enough in school to be admitted to a prestigious Ivy League college, but he kept to himself and had little to do with girls. He didn't actually discover his Jewish roots until he was in his first year of college. His parents had not only been totally secretive about their Jewish origins but had been openly anti-Semitic. They had bought into the WASP Mystique, that to be WASP was the only *acceptable* way to be. He too was anti-Semitic, until he was made aware of his roots, then became confused about his attitudes but some of his anti-Semitism persisted. He came into therapy with a terror of being found to be lacking and then discarded. It wasn't so much being discovered to be Jewish—in fact, as a journalist in New York most of his peers were Jewish. No, look to the mother, who had been a perfectionist, and part of being perfect in *her* view was *being* WASP and *not* being Jewish. Being so far short of his mother's view of perfection, it wasn't surprising that his ego was distinctly unstable, that he felt he was only as good as his last article and that at any moment he would be discovered to be a fraud and fired from his job. In fact, he was an outstanding success and grew in stature as a professional. In New York in the '70s and '80s it was difficult for an attractive successful young man *not* to have his pick of women. Nevertheless our man succeeded in failing—why should a woman like a man who so disliked himself? Eventually he got into a relationship with a WASP who was nearly as critical and demeaning of him as his mother had been. And then *she* left him.

Which was when he came into analysis with a female therapist. Over several years he came to feel genuinely accepted as a person by her. At first his relationships with women were very short ones. *He* would preempt the role of the critical parent and would quickly find physical or intellectual defects in them and dismiss them. At last he met a Jewish woman and tried to dismiss her too, but with the help of his analyst he was finally able to be married to her, and *by a rabbi,* coming out of the closet in front of his peers and friends. He still is shy and somewhat disparaging of others, but at least he has a clear insight into who and what he is and why he feels as he does, and in the process has shaken the WASP Mystique for a greater acceptance of himself and his Jewish origins.

Sarah was brought up in a small, affluent community in rural Delaware. She was a "Jewish princess" in many ways. Her father, a Russian immigrant, had been extremely successful in business. Sarah lived in a near-palace surrounded by acres of land with a private swimming pool, servants, Cadillacs. There was no hiding her father's Jewishness. He was a prototypical Eastern European Jew with a thick accent, a boisterous manner and no pretensions about being anything but himself.

Sarah's mother, however, was altogether different. She too was Jewish, but third generation. She was cultured, low-key and had a perfect WASP facade. She disparaged her husband's "bad" manners and "crude" speech and behavior. She played down her economic advantages, was WASPishly self-effacing—the worst sins in *her* book were to be showy or ostentatious—In short, to "look Jewish." This mother was actually prejudiced against her daughter Sarah because she—unlike her blue-eyed and blond mother—looked Jewish. She was dark, clearly Semitic with an expressive temperament much like her father's. Sarah grew up feeling miserably unattractive. She had no success with boys. Her mother openly admired the blond, blue-eyed WASP cheerleaders in her class and compared her unfavorably to them. Her father, a "male chauvinist," never could appreciate his daughter's intellect. Sarah, taking both extremes of a bad deal, incorporated her mother's and her father's perception of her. One might call it a double-whammy.

She managed to escape home by going to an out-of-town college, came to New York and began therapy. At the time she was anxious and disparaging of herself. But starting as a secretary in a literary agent's office, she rose to a top position in her field. After a disastrous marriage to a ne'er-do-well Jew who posed as a WASP, she had several affairs with WASP men. Ultimately she married the quintessential WASP and today has a good relationship with him. But despite continuing progress in therapy, Sarah still tends to disparage herself. She is also openly anti-Semitic, although she does not pretend *not* to be Jewish. Almost all her friends are WASPs, but she still feels insecure among people who are non-Jews and at the same time puts down Jews. She's nearly obsessive about sending her children to the best WASP schools, wanting her husband to look and act as WASP as possible (which as a WASP he can do without effort), dressing in understated fashion, having an apartment in the city and a house in the country—WASP country—all covertly denying her Jewishness.

After all, having a mother who at once says you are Jewish *and* that being Jewish is *no good and* only WASPs are acceptable is a series of hurdles difficult to negotiate and makes for a slow, slow change.

Sarah, Jack, Jane, Robert and the others . . . Jews not only accepting but at times in hot pursuit of presumed WASP superiority, they all suffered from an assault on their self-esteem. It's also true that this isn't simply a casual sequence. Being non-WASP didn't create the feeling of inferiority by itself. Much of it derived from the messages sent from parents to children about being less than acceptable as Jews. But the myth of WASP superiority served to provide a convenient place to put the blame on for the resulting feeling of worth-lessness, and at the same time, ironically and almost per-versely, helped absolve the parents. Was it their fault that in America WASP was most beautiful if you really wanted to be accepted?

All of which has a broader support throughout society. The mystique is pervasive, and belief in its mythology is hardly limited to Jews. The impact is not dissimilar among other ethnic minorities as well.

CHAPTER XIII

You Don't Have to Be Jewish to Pursue the Wasp Mystique

JOE was an American of Italian descent. Even though his grandfather, father and two of his uncles were successful doctors, his family persisted in a dim view of Italians and exalted WASPs. In the '20s and '30s the shortest book written was the Italo-American *Who's Who*. This was even before Joe DiMaggio's time. Fiorello LaGuardia was mayor of New York, but even that did not cut any ice since he was also part Jewish and in some ways seemed more a Texan than an Italian.

Joe's family was affluent. He went to the fancy WASP school down the block from his luxurious house. Yet his family still considered themselves "greenhorns." His grandparents and his father had been born in Italy and came over as poor immigrants, and never recovered from their original sense of humiliation and feeling of exclusion, all of which was passed on to Joe. The only regular guests at dinner were other Italians. Joe's father felt it an honor when a person of Irish, German or Jewish extraction would come. The notion of socializing with WASPs was too intimidating, and WASP doctors Joe's father came in contact with were spoken of in near-reverent terms, often all out of proportion to professional expertise. Joe's father was an equal in whites, but he didn't *feel* equal as a person.

At the fancy WASP school, sitting in a classroom next to the blond, blue-eyed daughter of the chairman of the board of a Fortune 500 corporation, Joe felt cruelly out of his element, felt inferior to his classmates. It didn't matter that they, in fact, didn't exclude him and that he was even elected class president. He rationalized this away on the basis of his being first academically, and so his ethnicity was *generously* overlooked. Joe had absorbed his parents' low evaluation of themselves, and of him.

He continued his record of academic excellence and was accepted at an Ivy League college, but at college his fantasy became a reality. Here he *was* excluded by the WASPs, and his only friends were Jews, Italians and the few Blacks, who were then called Negroes. Medical school would be a replay of college. Joe could never penetrate any WASP circles— though in truth, like his father, he never tried or was even open to such associations.

Meanwhile, Joe did have a series of WASP *girl* friends, dealing with his need to be accepted not by trying to crash the inner circle of WASP men but by conquering WASP women. He also reversed the imagined pain and humiliation of being excluded by them by abandoning them after he had won them and bragging that he had been with a woman from each of the so-called Seven Sisters colleges.

Only after years of psychoanalysis did Joe gradually begin to feel it was okay to be Italian. Trips to Italy and a built-in but long-denied appreciation of his cultural heritage helped him accept his origins. But it took a great deal to reverse the family message that it was *not* okay to be anything but WASP, and certainly not okay to be Italian. In spite of academic, professional and sexual successes, Joe's self-esteem is not very high—on a scale of one to ten about six, which is up from near zero. His parents and grandparents had taken in—been taken in by—the WASP values and thought of themselves with the disdain that WASP America had characteristically directed toward all immigrants, adjudged unfit for anything but ghettos and surely not qualified even to aspire to enter WASP territory.

Judy's situation is perhaps especially unusual because of the so-called visibility factor. She has a black father and a blue-eyed blond WASP mother, and while Judy is light brown she has identifiably Negroid features. Her mother's feelings about Blacks were ambivalent at best. Then why did she marry one? Perhaps to work out her own guilt about her supremely favored position in society *and* her own prejudice. But in addition to her guilt-producing prejudices she had some good objective reasons to feel hostility toward her husband—who was an alcoholic. So Judy became the victim of her WASP mother's prejudice against Blacks and her clear hostility toward her black husband, who in fact warranted what was felt. To say that Judy's self-esteem is, as it were, knee-high to a grasshopper is to exaggerate. She is, after all—not unlike Sarah—the victim of prejudice from her own mother!

Judy happened to be beautiful, creative and artistic, but most of her assets were dissipated in one way or another by an enormous self-hatred. She had taken in her mother's contempt for her blackness, which was, of course, reinforced by the attitude of society in general. She didn't know who she was or where she belonged. She was not accepted by Blacks because of her light color and her having incorporated many of her mother's WASP mannerisms and speech patterns. Her Black acquaintances called her "an uppity pretentious nigger." With her white friends she felt at a disadvantage because of her color, and assigned to them her mother's prejudice, whether they in fact had it or not.

Judy has the ability to compete as a sexual woman and also as a professional in her field of law. She is creative enough to be a writer. But mother's WASP facade and guilts, admixed with father's *genuine* defects, suffocated her assets and potential. Not a happy ending, but they all can't be and it would be dishonest to suggest otherwise. Therapy versus Mystique and family conditioning can be a loser.

Paul was brought up in a lower middle-class Italo-American home in a small city in upper New York. His father was a pretentious fellow, dressed sharply and was self-aggrandiz-ing, but he was a flop in his financial ventures. His mother, also Italo-American, liked to read "American" magazines and tried to dress and act like what she perceived to be an Ameri-can lady despite her limited resources. Paul's family were the storied "poor relations." During the Depression his father lost his job, the family could not pay the rent and he and his parents had to stay at the home of somewhat better off but unpretentious "lower-class" Italo-American relatives who not surprisingly took the opportunity to make fun of his parents and the "airs they put on." For Paul it was a time of humiliation. His parents, who liked to act as if they were "Americanized," became the butt of jokes about lower-class Italians.

Paul decided he'd had enough of humiliation and wanted none of his parents'. By enormous hard work, diligence and talent he made it through college, got on the corporate ladder and in a short time became one of the brightest lights in his company. (No, *not* Lee Iacocca.) He made several hundred thousand dollars a year, lived in fine mansions in the best WASP neighborhoods, sent his sons to the best WASP prep schools and had all the external accoutrements of success.

But Paul spent every day of his life in a kind of panic. He felt he was a fraud, an imposter who would be unmasked at any moment, as his father had been. He wore Brooks Broth-ers suits, drove a Mercedes, lived and looked like a WASP, but underneath was the poor Italian boy from a poor family in a poor neighborhood who was pulling the emotional strings. Despite his professional successes he feared his whole structure would collapse at any moment and he would be unmasked. Rather than feeling pride about having risen from and above his humble origins, he persisted in feeling shame and humiliation about them.

So the acceptance of the WASP Mystique—that *they* are the cultural and moral superiors—has its impact on members of a variety of minority groups who aspire to be part of the socioeconomic elite. The WASP standards—those of the ruling class in America—are still very much the national standards for an elite group. Minority people try to take on these standards, even if they consciously disavow them and even make fun of them. They also don't quite feel that they're okay because of their cultural and ethnic backgrounds. Why not? Because they're different from the original and most distinguishable minority of them all—The American WASPs, who started as demeaned dissidents and immigrants, and got to the top fast by an accident of history, not inherent worth. So-called minorities should try to keep this in mind.

CHAPTER XIV

Even Wasps Want to Be More Like Wasps

A WASP friend was sitting in a restaurant when an acquaintance from her set walked in and sat down at the table next to her. She was sparkling and vivacious but the friend found her laugh most disturbing. She said that it was a phony tinkling kind of laugh that came at every third sentence or so regardless of what was being said. It was as if she were exhibiting her social graces, her charisma and her wit and clearly announcing to all that she was very much a member of the elite inner circle. In the process she stirred up some old but powerful conflicts for our friend, so much so that she had to leave the restaurant. She felt that she was inferior to this woman because she couldn't display the same so charming facade so effortlessly. At the same time, unaware of the contradiction, she said she felt superior to this "phony empty woman who was all tinsel and no substance." One of her friends, she said, had described such a woman as "underneath all that tinsel there is more tinsel." Feeling inferior and superior to another person at the same time is not very good for the digestion—ergo, the quick exit from her unfinished meal.

Our friend had been brought up in a modest but comfortable home in one of the most affluent WASP communities in the country. She was, however, surrounded by homes that were like castles compared to her home, and her neighbors measured their property in square miles rather than acres. She had never felt able to compete in this league, and at the same time felt superior to those "pretentious" types. Even though her family was wealthy and socially exalted by almost anybody else's standards, they always felt they paled in comparison to their neighbors . . .

So even WASPs want to be more like WASPs.

As mentioned, prominent among WASP values is always needing to strive to come closer to the WASP ideal, being very self-critical, looking up to one's betters as well as looking down on all others. Even if one is considered by outsiders as up and in, there is always someone who is *more* up and in who is looking down on one critically. And the way one maintains one's tenuous perch is always to have someone else to look down on.

So the good WASP must go through life on the edge, feeling his acceptability among the elite of *his* elite always on the line. One is only as good as one's last performance, and each new situation requires another performance. For WASPs in particular, new situations are not likely to be filled with anticipation of pleasure so much as the fear of humiliation and exposure. For too many, "the lights are on but there's nobody home." There's a tremulous reliance on the false self, which tends to make a new encounter or venture something not to be desired. When new situations can be avoided, they mostly are avoided. To do otherwise can create tension, strain, anxiety.

We hear throughout the media about the lack of competitiveness in American business vis-à-vis its foreign competitors. Some of the blame has gone to a putatively over-valued dollar, to cheap foreign labor, to restrictive duties put on American goods, et cetera. Maybe all these have their roles, but underlying them is the quintessentially WASPish demeanor and approach to life among those captains of industry, whether *actually* WASP or not, who run most of America's major businesses. What really is their motto? To build a better mouse trap and for less than the other fellow? Hardly. It's to "maximize earning for the shareholders," to wipe out competition by swallowing the competition, often with appropriately named "junk bonds," and to bail out in the event of failure by way of "greenmail" and/or a "white knight" to save one's skin and protect one's special emoluments known, appropriately, as "golden parachutes." Be proper, don't rock the boat, get along by going along, stay, for *God's* sake, a respected member of the club and for *heaven's* sake avoid being peculiar or eccentric or too individualistic—all of which connote more recent arrivals on these shores—

including, of course, the original WASP, who has long since lost his sting but still sets the style and tone and objectives for the nation as a whole—the WASP Mystique rampant on a shield of eminent RESPECTABILITY and SENSE OF BELONGING.

Maintaining this facade, regardless of the juices that may perk below, can take its toll. Those—even bank presidents—who would like to act against the code rarely are able to. They have been brought up in a culture that tends to disparage their "true selves" and reward their "false selves." Even if it makes them feel like imposters, once they have developed a set of behaviors that is *acceptable,* they cling to it tenaciously, play it, literally, close to the vest. And yet they can never be sure that, careful as they may be, some aspect of their true selves, some *unacceptable* aspect that will result in being shunned and disparaged and thrown out of the club, will show through. The result will be humiliation, mostly in their *own* eyes, and will push them even deeper into hiding.

So even being a literal WASP is not enough because the facade may not be WASP enough and what's behind it may be distinctly at variance with WASP values. And if these values add to a mystique, which means they don't really exist in objective reality, how can one possibly live up to them?

Pity the poor WASP, who can never be WASP enough.

STING OF THE WASP

CHAPTER XV

Prejudice Among Wasps

ARE WASPs prejudiced? Is prejudice an important component of their psyches? Whom is the prejudice directed toward? Is it open or covert?

Let's define prejudice. In the context of this book it means the disparagement of other ethnic groups and individuals whose values are contrary to the values of the WASP Mystique. WASPs, as suggested in the last chapter, have been known to discriminate against their own kind if, for example, their political beliefs go against traditional WASP conservatism. Take Archie Bunker (although some claim he's a put-on). He feels his ethnic group is superior to others. Archie, however, is a lower middle-class WASP, not well educated or "refined." What about upper-class WASPs? Are they prejudiced? As Archie might say, yes, and in spades. Archie, many feel, expresses his mindless prejudice in "truly tasteless jokes" and other gross behavior. The upper-class WASPs do it more subtly. Their public position is to eschew prejudice, to denounce it as unfair and indeed immoral. They often head up political and social organizations dedicated to the fight against prejudice. WASPs are extremely cautious about overt expressions of prejudice. They tend to be taken aback by tasteless jokes, especially if expressed in the presence of mixed company—mixed being not so much the ladies but company of undiscernible ethnic makeup. In the safe precincts of their own homes or clubs they can be the most shamelessly mischievous, to put it kindly, joke-tellers. But in public they maintain their stance of moral superiority by denouncing any overt expressons of prejudice. Tacky, old boy.

It's often said that education and prejudice are conversely related; the better-educated a person is the less likely he or she is to be prejudiced. Not true. Most WASPs are reasonably well educated. Actually education can, in one sense, make it easier to be prejudiced if one is so disposed because people learn how to be more discreet about the prejudicial feelings they may have. No, unfortunately, education does not eliminate prejudice—which is a deep emotional response rather than an intellectual one.

WASPs don't express their prejudice by overt attacks or vilification. Rather it's expressed in the typical upper-class WASP manner of veiled contempt and shunning. On a personal level—among the boys on the "nineteenth" hole or at a dinner party or in the boardroom—it is more likely to be expressed with more overt humor, accompanied by a know-ing smile and a wink. In the most general way, though, it works through exclusion—by not letting minority people into their neighborhood or club. Recently there was surprise to discover that Supreme Court Justice Rehnquist owned a home in which the deed prevented it being sold to Blacks or Jews. Granted as claimed it was an oversight, but to some a serious one. In the fifties Laura Hobson's *Gentleman's Agreement* dramatized the exclusionary policy of many hotels, clubs and resorts vis-à-vis Jews. But this policy, unspoken, continues in force in many WASP clubs and neighborhoods and businesses. The upper-class WASP way is not to jump in and join up with the Ku Klux Klan or the American Nazi party. Their prejudice operates through shunning and exclu-sion and avoidance rather than direct attack. And the result is far more invidious. It also fills the bill of allowing them to maintain their position of moral superiority by overtly condemning prejudice while secretly and privately holding to their own prejudices—which, granted, may be uncon-scious.

WASPs self-protectively avoid coming into conflict with their often unaware feelings of prejudice by avoiding the objects of their prejudice. They try not to dirty their hands or their psyches. Consider Bert, a young WASP lawyer, who remembers bringing home a Jewish friend from high school. He recalls how his mother asked the boy his last name, not belligerently, but more as though out of politeness to get it right. She got it, and never said another word to him after she heard the distinctly Jewish name. She just ignored both of them while this person was visiting. Her message clearly got across to Bert, who never invited the Jewish boy over again. Silence was a weapon of prejudice, and a reflection of contempt.

Too many of us—but it would seem WASPs in particular—are stuck at a stage where there's an imbalance between the critic, the judging superego, and one's thoughts and behavior. So there's a tendency to be very critical of behavior one can't help but indulge in, but doesn't approve of. There's a constant barrage from conscience, critical parents, for being bad children. The alternative is not to do what one really would like to do in order to be a good child and satisfy the critical parent. This diminishes guilt but it also builds inhibitions and frustrations of gratification, including some creative ones.

All this is essentially the way things work within the individual and explains a good deal about WASP guilt and inhibitions. Among individuals the mechanism is that much bruited-about projection. One projects either the bad child *or* the critical parent onto another person or group. If one projects the critical parent then one feels subjected to their critical, moralistic judgment. One feels like a bad child doing wrong or wrong thinking or both. One feels guilty and bad, which is the way many WASPs do feel in relation to their mates, their parents, their bosses, their church or their community.

The other and probably more palatable interpersonal solution is to take on the role of the critical, morally superior parent and project the bad child onto one's mate, parent, boss or other person or group. Which is where prejudice and scapegoating come in. If one can find the appropriate person or group to play out the role of the bad child, then one can play the role of the critical parent and try to avoid one's own guilt and self-criticism by making some "other" the victim of one's rebukes.

Since WASPs perhaps more than other ethnic groups have the alternative of being either the morally reprehensible child or the critical, morally superior adult they will obviously choose the latter as often as possible. And if they can identify another person or ethnic group as being the bad child or children lacking in proper moral fiber, then they can get off the hook of being in that position themselves. From which follows the WASPs' tendency to set themselves up in a superior position—the natural breeding ground for prejudice.

And toward whom is upper-class WASP prejudice directed and what's the "basis" of this prejudice? Well, WASPs have the usual amount of prejudice toward Blacks, Hispanics, Italians, Poles and Irish. But these groups don't really fill the bill, don't threaten them with claims or demonstrations of moral or financial superiority. Prejudice against these groups is too easy, like a football player's "cheap shot" at an unprotected opponent. The major target of WASP prejudice clearly is and always was destined to be the Jews. Jews have a solid historical basis for being in the position of victims. They also strongly and proudly assert the moral and ethical superiority of their beliefs. They too are engaged in numerous charitable activities that thereby threaten the WASP's exclusive claim on noblesse oblige. They are often in the vanguard of activities against prejudice, defamation, social inequities and injustice. From a WASP perspective, they make a very strong attempt—in spite of their relatively small numbers in terms of the general population—to invade if not preempt the WASP's closely and dearly held position of moral superiority. And they also make strong inroads into WASP territories of money and power, all very threatening to WASP positions.

So what better target for WASP prejudice than the Jews? Rather than the WASPs' feeling guilty for their exploitation and victimization of minorities and misuse of their money and power, the WASPs can turn this around. They can make the Jews the exploiters of money and power. And they have their jokes to capsulize this—"The shortest book ever written is *Jewish Business Ethics,*" and other ethnic jokes that put Jews down for their alleged displays of money and power. Such jokes, reflecting prejudice, are intended to knock the Jews off their perch of being the morally superior victims and put the WASPs back into that position. And so in the process now *they* are the victims of the Jews' misuse of their power, they can reestablish the position of being the critical, morally superior parent and put the Jews back into the role of the bad child.

An interesting light on all this comes from considering what happens when a WASP enters psychotherapy with a Jewish therapist. An acquaintance told one of the authors of this book that she had given up on psychotherapy. None of the therapists she had seen shared her white Anglo-Saxon background. She also complained that her lifestyle was paralyzing her. Her life might look great on the surface but she was unhappy and she just couldn't seem to get her point across to *anyone*. Was the reason for this, she wondered, because she was such a prototypical WASP? She figured that maybe she could get some help if she could find someone who seemed like her on the surface but had experienced the same discontentment—ideally another WASP, except WASPs were the last people willingly to express their feelings about anything. So she couldn't even talk to her closest friends. As for professional help, most of the therapists she had seen had been Jewish and she would bring this up in her initial interviews with them as a potential problem. In the end she gave up because she felt her worry about the difference in ethnic backgrounds was being interpreted as an expression of prejudice rather than legitimate concern. She felt too intimidated to ask for a referral, figuring this would further substantiate the therapist's interpretation that she was prejudiced. She could not tolerate being accused of prejudice—that, after all, was for people with inferior values to her.

Our initial reaction to this woman's complaint was not too sympathetic. We thought she *was* prejudiced. Her lifestyle was enviable to the authors—an American dream come true. She was well educated and thanks to her husband's visibility in the financial world potentially influential. Our reaction evolved into one of personal envy and professional pity mixed, frankly, with some arrogance. It seemed unlikely that if she really wanted to get some help she couldn't get any sort of counseling and counsel she wanted. She hardly seemed a victim, though from her point of view she was. A paradox, that she of all people should feel shut out, yet she did because she couldn't acknowledge even the possibility that *she* was prejudiced, might be just like any other fallible human being, including a therapist. This would take her out of her WASP-ish victim-mode, compromise her dearly held illusion of moral superiority, so central to the WASP Mystique.

CHAPTER XVI

Wasp Envy

ENVY is a major component of what minority group members, including WASPs who aren't part of the WASP elite, must feel about the WASP elite. It's a corrosive feeling directed against someone who possesses merely by being born into the right family; that's the ultimate in unfair competition.

There are three fairly typical defenses against this envy that apply to the majority who aren't in the WASP elite. The two most prominent are idealization on the one hand, and devaluing one's self on the other. There's little question that elite WASPs tend to be idealized by the rest of the population. Imitation is the sincerest form of flattery, and we've seen how strongly, urgently and persistently WASP manners, clothing, behavior and tastes are the style-setters for the rest of the population. Devaluing one's self—we've seen it repeatedly in the examples we've given—is what so many non-WASPs who aspire to join the elite tend to do, putting themselves down, never feeling as good as the WASP that's envied. In the process it's a way of rationalizing acceptance of one's lot. If you haven't got it, how in the world can you even begin to have notions of being as good as the best? So why bother?

The third defense, devaluing the envied person or group, is, quite remarkably, a rarity. There are endless "Truly Tasteless Jokes" about Italians, Poles, Blacks, Jews and other minorities. There are almost *no* jokes that devalue the WASP. The authors made an effort to collect WASP jokes but were able to come up with only four: How many WASPs does it take to change a lightbulb? Two. One to screw in the bulb, the other one to make the martinis . . . How can you tell when a WASP woman has an orgasm? She drops her *New Yorker* . . . Why do WASP women avoid orgies? They can't cope with writing all those thank-you notes . . . What's the definition of a WASP? Someone who gets out of the shower to tinkle.

Pretty thin stuff, we agree, relatively tame, non-disparaging, benign. Jokes against the ruling class have traditionally been numerous and vicious and vulgar. Rome is full of anti-clerical jokes. In America, jokes are mostly about its minorities, not about its ruling class. Envy of WASPs is dealt with almost exclusively by idealization and devaluation of the self—almost never be devaluing *them*. Once again, it seems to follow the British system in which the upper classes, especially the Royal Family and associated Royals, are held in near-worshipful esteem by those beneath them. Maybe it has to do in part with the perpetuation of the myth that the upper classes are somehow morally superior, else how did they get to be upper? More likely the major reason WASP values are so relatively immune to attack has to do with their values dictating that the good WASP is invisible rather than visible, modest rather than grandiose, frugal rather than conspicuous-consuming, quiet rather than loud or even outspoken, self-effacing rather than ostentatious or prideful, self-contained rather than expressive. Antimatter is harder to attack than matter. A reclusive target is hard to hit, and by its remoteness takes on an aura to inspire respect, fear and even awe. Most definitely the stuff of which mystiques are made.

CHAPTER XVII

Wasps and the Search for Soul

"SOUL" in America is usually left to Afro-Americans. WASPs, as usual, are looking for roles, formulas for behavior. Bruno Bettelheim once wrote an article for *The New Yorker* that was subsequently transformed into a book. The major point of the article was that English translations of Freud, done mostly in America, had taken the soul out of psychoanalysis. He meant this literally as well as figuratively. It seems the German word for "soul" was translated as "psyche," which is much closer to "mind." This, among other changes in nuances in American translations, produced a change in the sense of the meaning of the psychoanalytic process. It made what had begun as a search for soul and spirit into a search for scientific formulations and rules of behavior.

So psychoanalysis, which began as a search for one's unique, individual spirit or soul, has in America been reduced to discovering a set of formulas and rules for *fitting* into our society. How WASP-like can you get? Even the psychoanalysts have been bitten by the WASP Mystique. Interestingly enough, not even in England—the mother country of the WASP—did psychoanalysis take the same turn. English psychoanalysts—Klein, Bowlby, Fairbairn, Winnicott, Guntrip and others—focused their attention on the emotional interaction between mother and child. Their interest was in studying the interpersonal relationships that either bolstered or threatened one's sense of security. Given the matriarchal archetype of the British family and the Queen as their society's social model, this was a fitting adaptation of psychoanalysis to its cultural context. The British had a more practical attitude toward the application of psychoanalysis that did not necessarily include the more spiritual search for meaning and understanding that the Germans were responsible for.

In the United States psychoanalytic theory has been addressing only half the problem—the maladjustment of the individual. This sort of rather fatalistic approach may well be what underpins the pejorative term "shrink" if all we are really doing is trying to fit a lot of square pegs into a round hole. In any case, psychoanalysis has had to suffer its own growing pains as it has tried to expand beyond its original focus on sexuality during the Victorian period.

Americans have taken the British trend toward practicality one step further in their application of psychoanalysis and have turned it almost entirely into a tool to aid in social adaptation. American psychoanalysis isn't in its mainstream really interested in freeing the soul or increasing one's ability for expression. As a result a number of factions have broken off from traditional psychoanalysis in its Americanized version that tends to be decidedly less orthodox than the standard, prevailing American interpretation of Freudian psychoanalysis. What's more, in their fashion these factions seem closer to Freud's original aim than mainstream American psychoanalysis.

Perhaps the psychoanalyst who came closest to viewing psychoanalysis as the search for the soul was Jung, a Swiss. His approach paid little attention to the patient's adjustment to his family, his subculture or larger society. Part of his focus was on the so-called collective unconscious—groups of racial memories passed on in the unconscious from generation to generation. These consisted of various myths and symbols that appeared repeatedly in the art and literature of one race in contrast to another.

The designation of the matriarch as an unconsciously accepted symbol in WASP culture is an example of a Jungian archetype passed down from generation to generation and surviving even a trip across the Atlantic when the British transplanted themselves to America. Much of WASP behavior lends itself to a Jungian interpretation since it has traditionally been a tightly in-bred culture.

But Jung has suffered from criticism in America; he has been accused of being a racist and a Nazi-sympathizer even though he was in no way interested in politics. Jung was dedicated to the exploration of the spirit, which is the prime reason for his lack of popularity and skeptical reception in America. He was *impractical*. His attention was focused on man's relationship to himself, to God and to the universe rather than on his adaptation to his surroundings or mundane, practical life. Jung was very much interested in religion, especially in Eastern religions. Jungian analysts have often been criticized for not paying attention to the individual's relationships to his mate, his children, his neighbors or the society in which he lives—although a thorough-going Jungian analysis could not help but affect all of these relationships, even if indirectly. A Jungian would probably acknowledge his lack of attention to such issues but would also say that they are not the substance of the psychoanalytic process. Freud himself disowned Jung as being too mystical and religious. Jung, after all, threatened Freud's premise—that man is fundamentally motivated by his sexuality. While also interested in freeing the spiritual part of us, Freud took a more scientific approach to understanding man's behavior. In doing so he expected to uncover the unconscious fantasy life, which is still closer to the spiritual side than American psychoanalysis recognizes.

Adjustment is where the emphasis lies in traditional psychoanalysis, American style, which excludes WASPs, however unintentionally, because if anything WASPs are *over-*adjusted. Yet WASPs still can suffer from feeling they don't fit in, just as every other ethnic group does. The difference is that non-WASPs can't accept a WASP feeling unhappy in the same way they can other ethnic groups. The WASP

Mystique, with its illusion of superiority and invulnerability, pretty well rules it out. We tend to look on WASPs as beyond the problems of ordinary mortals. They are the ultimate of American society at its "well-adjusted best."

Though many of the prominent psychoanalysts in America emigrated from Europe, they seem to have changed the focus of psychoanalysis once they reached America. They too were smitten by the WASP Mystique. Sandor Rado based his analytic system on adaptation. Margaret Mahler focused her attention on the process of separation that occurs between mother and child. Erik Erikson described the different stages a person goes through from birth to death. Alfred Adler's attention was on the individual's compensating for organic or other inferiorities and his striving for power. Erich Fromm explored the meaning of love in relationships. Karen Horney concentrated on the effects of cultural forces on the formation of the neurotic personality. Adolf Meyer's psychobiology was based on connecting symptoms with past experiences. Freida Fromm-Reichman explored the relationship between the patient and the analyst.

All were famous American analysts European-born and trained. None was particularly interested in exploring the soul. They were joined by American-born analysts who shared their emphasis. Harry Stack Sullivan, for example, was mostly interested in interpersonal relationships. Clara Thompson studied the impact of cultural forces on the individual. It's interesting that no Jungian or Rankian analyst achieved special popularity or fame in the United States.

America's analysts, clearly influenced by the WASP Mystique, have become more and more involved in helping their patients fit into their environment—an important WASP value. Family therapy is a very American institution, almost trendy, that tries to help people adjust to their nuclear and extended families. Ego psychology—also a very American creation—puts maximum value on getting along in the outside world. WASP America, as we know, is very much about fitting the individual into his subculture and into the culture as a whole.

American psychoanalysis has, it seems, become a tool of the WASP Mystique without even recognizing the transformation. Psychoanalysis seems to have lost its soul on being imported into America, just as many WASPs have had to give up their selves—and with their selves their souls—in order to defend the most civilized, if also stultifying, traditions of American society.

CHAPTER XVIII

Wasps, Politics and Change, Including Women and Yuppies

WASPS, then, like psychoanalysis, which along with most of America has bought their mystique, are well if not wisely anchored. The WASP is keenly sensitive to any new movement or thought that might even in the slightest rock his boat. So by nature and presumed necessity he is conservative, a self-preservationist rather than a self-fulfiller. The majority of WASPs are Republicans and lean more toward conservative than liberal thought, though many WASPs would consider themselves liberal. WASPs often have a well-developed social conscience and are sympathetic toward liberal views, at least in theory. It's when they are put into practice that they tend to pose a problem for WASPs—it can, after all, cramp their lifestyle. When it comes down to it, WASPs prefer to keep government out of their lives and most especially out of their pockets. So generally, and at the bottom line, WASPs and liberal politics just don't mix very well.

WASP conservatism shows itself off particularly when it is challenged by progressive intellectual movements. WASPs tend to cast a disapproving eye on the influence of psychoanalytic thought and to deny that it has had major impact on our society. Psychoanalysis is threatening to WASPs because it is, in a sense, the granddaddy of America's preoccupation with self-help. America is a country that likes to believe in the possibility of self-realization, self-fulfillment, even though it may have to compromise along the way. WASPs can't afford to believe in such a premise; for generations they have been putting their energy into sustaining *their* standard of social adjustment. To entertain seriously such a notion would mean abandoning all the values WASPs are raised on, to redefine their rigid notion of self. This would be a painful process, with WASPs having to admit that all their lives they were living under the misassumption that the self has no will of its own independent of how it's *supposed* to be perceived by others. If a child has been raised to believe that children should be seen and not heard, then as an adult he will have lived his whole life in reference to the direction and stimulus of others. Admitting this, let alone *changing* it, could lead to a profound depression over all the time wasted living one's life according to the program of others.

So the WASP takes this program, the set of values he has been raised on, into himself and they become himself, inseparable from who he is as a person. That WASPs are conservative is, then, perhaps not so much a political statement as it is a personal statement about how they must protect themselves from the influence of others whose beliefs and values might be different from their own and thereby threaten to undermine them.

It's not uncommon for WASPs to feel they are being invaded, since they also, at their upper echelon, tend to own inherited property. When an invader hovers in view—a *parvenu* non-WASP, Black, Jewish, Italian, whatever—it's not difficult to mobilize the rest of the WASP community by subtly appealing to their prejudices, which are deeply ingrained, invoking such euphemisms as quality of the area, zoning laws, overdevelopment, and so forth. The WASP's territory like his values can't be separated from who he is as a person. He is defined by the community that surrounds him and if that community changes, then he must change. He will not do this without tremendous resistance.

The woman's movement, like psychoanalysis, is an arena WASPs are predisposed to turn their backs on. Ironically it is WASP women more than WASP men who have perpetuated WASP resistance to feminism. Not surprising. The female WASP is guaranteed a certain amount of power if she remains a traditional WASP wife who busies herself strengthening the family's ties while her husband works. If she too goes to work she must give up her role as the matriarch and with it unconditional respect for being the self-sacrificing mother who always puts her family before herself. There's more in it for her to remain unemployed, at home, and reap vicariously the benefits of her spouse's and her children's success in the world. It's through them, their works and the family's social connections that the family will be guaranteed social standing in the future. The traditionally reared female WASP tends to understand from early childhood that it is how she is perceived by society rather than her own personal accomplishments and achievements that are of personal worth to her. She would be left floundering if she were not tied to her family, generation after generation. To acknowledge, never mind embrace, the movement toward greater independence for women would mean to become more dependent on society rather than her family. This goes against all her history and tradition. With notable exceptions, she is programmed otherwise.

Status quo, and the security that presumably goes with it, are near-biblical tenets for WASPs—and those who would be.

An elderly WASP gentleman commented at a cocktail party that his family was falling apart because his grandchildren were all preoccupied with their "obsessive self-help" routines. He couldn't understand why they were choosing to question the "obvious" security that would be provided for them by the traditions and, in their case, the affluence of their WASP family. They answer that the status quo ain't what it used to be, which requires they try to figure out where they belong.

Once upon a time one could expect to find a WASP at the top of the corporate masthead. Now, heaven forbid, there are folks whose surnames end in vowels. The old-boy network can no longer absolutely guarantee their sons a rocking chair atop corporate America as a birthright.

One should take care not to overstate this appearance of democratization, some might say mongrelization, these cracks in the ethnic boardroom walls. Scan the lists of CEO's of publicly held corporations and they are still predominated by discernibly WASP names. True, some of those names may have started out as something else, having been changed along the way to sound unassailably WASP. Which further proves the point. The mystique is still there: to be WASP is to rule, to be or seem to be WASP is to be worthy of rule and to have the best chance of making it in America.

The message has come across loud and clear to those thousands of eager young men and women who yearly pour out of the graduate schools with their MBAs shining bright. They may seem like threats to the elderly gentlemen mentioned above, but viewed another way, they perhaps should be reassuring to him—they are, after all, taking the values of the mystique that his family and those before it have established, and doing their level best to imitate the elite in every way—from superficials of dress and speech to vocation and residence to political and even religious persuasion.

Americans are still associating WASP ethics and appearances with power without defining and evaluating power. Is it social status that accords one a position of power or is it economic? WASPs prefer to believe it is social, though even for WASPs it was originally economic. WASPs prefer to believe that they have been in a position of power because of *who* and *what* they are. Andrew Carnegie said God gave me my money, and he believed it. After all, *anyone* can become economically powerful in this country. Clearly goodness and divine beneficence shine on those most deserving to be superior—the gospel according to WASP, largely swallowed whole by the rest of America as the WASP Mystique.

Power is not something to be complacent about—once it's in place it must always be defended. Feeling powerful depends at least in part on others to validate the values we've chosen to live by and the lifestyles that express those values. The shortest path to a position of power has been to accept and pattern one's life after the traditional values of the WASP ethics that dominated our economic development and put us as a nation in a position of power. The grandchildren of the elderly WASP gentleman may be getting restless, but they are still probably a minority. And their non-WASP counterparts are very much carrying on the faith.

One refers to the aggressive and upwardly mobile mass of young individuals who have generically come to be known as Yuppies. Relative to their age, they tend to be politically conservative and traditional in their values. Their lives are a celebration of "The American Way," and their lifestyles and values are reminiscent of the pre-Vietnam unquestioning go-along-get-along approach of the '50s. Yuppies express themselves through the hot pursuit of economic success, which presumably will lead to a greater independence, a position from which they can perhaps be more truly self-expressive and, one hopes, shed the constraints of Yuppiedom.

Unfortunately things don't always work out. Once the Yuppie, like the WASP, acquires a certain amount of wealth and financial security, he puts himself in the position of having to defend that security. The greater the amount of time and energy put into defending something already in place, the less reserve left over for freely expressing oneself. At the beginning the choices seem sound; responsible choices within the context of the society one lives in. But in the end they often can and do lead to a feeling of entrapment, even as we've seen is the case with many successful WASP businessmen. And entrapment, of course, is the antithesis of independence, which was the motivating force behind WASP economic prosperity just as it is for the modern-day Yuppie.

It's perhaps not accurate to label this social transition a neo-conservative movement without examining the forces that set it into motion. Americans are still, fundamentally, a people in search of independence, and neo-conservatism is less of a movement than a reaction to not having yet found a better way.

We need to remind ourselves that as a country we are barely out of our infancy. Our accepted norm created by the WASP Mystique is not set in the concrete of ages. It just sometimes seems that way. It won't be easy to liberate us from the WASP Mystique, but a greater understanding of what it is and how it works can go a long way, we trust, toward that end. We started out as a nation fighting for liberation and its fruit of liberty. Our bet is that we've only just begun to fight.

Postscript

THE impact of the WASP Mystique with its emphasis on the apparent over the real goes national and international. We elect actors as our President and law-makers. We vote not so much for the person as for the image he portrays. Warren G. Harding, a pol of little talent, was elected president because he *looked* like a president. Thomas E. Dewey was defeated because he *looked* like the man at the top of a wedding cake. Ronald Reagan *looks* like a macho, forthright, capable man in charge of himself and his life. Politicians pay public relations firms millions of dollars to create the right image for the public, and aren't embarrassed to admit it. John F. Kennedy, it is said with some reason, defeated Richard Nixon because he came off *looking* better in their television debates. He was young, handsome and charismatic; Nixon was dour, sweaty and five-o'clock-shadowed. Never mind the issues and one's articulation of them, the winners of political races tend to be those who have the qualities that add to a charismatic image—in short, the ones who can best play a role, and whose values at least *appear* to exemplify the mystique of WASPism.

We tend to buy the image, not the person. When we discover that a Gary Hart is unfaithful, that a president's sexual adventures made Don Juan's dalliances pale, that even a Martin Luther King had some clay in his feet, we are thrown off kilter. We have signed on for their personas. When their complete, true selves appear and we discover they are humanly fallible, we get angry and reject them. We seem to prefer an image to the real thing—a legend to a living reality. We love the obfuscation of the mystique so long as it reassures us in our preconceptions.

This seems a particularly American and British phenomenon. Can you imagine a reporter asking Charles de Gaulle if he had ever been unfaithful? Le Grande Charles would have picked him up and thrown him out of the room. Other world leaders were known to have strayed. But when Gary Hart falls he is forced to withdraw as a candidate. Similarly for British Cabinet ministers who fall from grace. There is a part of us—perhaps a built-in corrective—that seems to enjoy destroying icons, these false images, and at last seeing the person behind the facade; the politician who is a liar and philanderer, the sports hero who is a wife-beater and drug addict, the movie star whose private life would make

Caligula blush, the "charismatic" evangelist who lies, steals and philanders.

And there are no boundaries to the phenomenon. In our foreign affairs, we too often seem to be jettisoning the fine principles we have long given lip-service to in favor of the Marxist-Leninist doctrine, the very centerpiece of Communist ideology, that the ends justify the means. We have the spectacle of a Marine officer, his secretary, an admiral, all evoking the doctrine that there is something above the law when the rightness of the ends as perceived by certain individuals and groups so dictates. Does this sound familiar? It should, because it also has the ring of the supervening superiority of the mystique of the WASP and its claim to a moral ascendancy justifying its preeminence in our society for WASPs and their multitude of pretenders.

Without getting involved in partisanship, we suggest it is fairly clear that on most every front—personal, national, international—America is involved in preserving and fostering images rather than facing up to and dealing with the reality of the matter, however painful and anxiety-making the process may be.

But as we suggested at the end of the last chapter of this book, there is a movement afoot, fueled by a restless uneasiness, that mystiques and images can be runaways of destruction to the individual, society at large and the national welfare. "Why don't I feel better if everything is so wonderful?" asked Congressman Dante B. Fascell at the recent Iran-Contra hearings. Although his and other voices may have less volume and coverage than some others, they nevertheless are beginning to be heard. They express a rejection of image and mystique, and a willingness—even a cleansing desire—to go behind and beyond the graven images, WASP or otherwise, and get us back to what we really are and can be—individually and nationally.